HOUSE *of* GLORY

FINDING PERSONAL MEANING
IN THE TEMPLE

S. MICHAEL WILCOX

DESERET BOOK COMPANY
SALT LAKE CITY, UTAH

Photographs of temples in order of appearance: Kirtland Temple, Swiss
Temple, Sydney Australia Temple, Tokyo Temple, Washington Temple,
Mexico City Temple, Johannesburg South Africa Temple, San Diego
California Temple.

Photographs © The Church of Jesus Christ of Latter-day Saints. Used by
permission.

Visit us at deseretbook.com

Library of Congress Cataloging-in-Publication Data

    Wilcox, S. Michael.
      House of glory : finding personal meaning in the temple / S. Michael
Wilcox.
      p.   cm.
    Includes bibliographical references and index.
    ISBN 0-87579-970-1
    1. Temple endowments (Mormon Church)   2. Mormon temples.
3. Spiritual life—Mormon Church.   I. Title.
BX8643.T4W55   1995
246'.9589332—dc20   95-8719
                                                               CIP

Printed in the United States of Americ   72076
Publishers Printing, Salt Lake City, UT

20   19   18   17   16   15   14

Contents

PART 6: HOUSE OF THANKSGIVING

"The Luckiest Boy"

Recently I returned to my boyhood home of San Bernardino, California. As I walked down the streets reflecting on my youth, many thoughts and emotions returned. I remembered all the insecurities and fears of my youth, especially those associated with my teenage years. I was small and often the object of bullying by boys older and bigger than I. During those years I did not consider myself as being very lucky, and I often envied others whose accomplishments or advantages seemed so desirable. I thought, "Thank heaven those days are over; I would not like to relive them again." I suppose I gave way to a good dose of self-pity.

My reflections continued for some time along these lines until finally the Spirit whispered a surprising and wholly unexpected truth. "You were the luckiest boy ever to grow up in San Bernardino," the Spirit said. The words came so powerfully and clearly that I could not mistake the source, but I did not believe the words that were spoken. "Not so! Not so!" I answered. "I was not the luckiest boy! How could I have been, considering all the experiences I remember?"

Once again, clear and strong, came the Spirit's peaceful voice: "You had the fullness of the gospel of Jesus Christ and a mother who knew it was true!" As I received this truth, I saw my youth clearly for the first time in my life. I was in reality the luckiest boy who ever grew up in San Bernardino, California, but I could not have accepted this truth until my life had shown me all the glorious aspects of the Savior's light.

This book is about only one ray of that light, that of the holy temple. It is a ray I have come to love deeply. If, among all the wonderful, edifying subjects that belong to the gospel, all I ever knew was the temple, I would still have been the luckiest and most blessed boy. Its blessings alone are sufficient to render us all the most blessed people to inhabit the earth. That we receive so many other blessings with it is but a testimony of the grace and mercy of a compassionate and loving Father in Heaven. Against the backdrop of all the glorious blessings of the gospel, the temple stands out, to use Joseph Smith's words, as "this most glorious of all subjects belonging to the everlasting gospel." (D&C 128:17.)

I do not have a sufficient gift to describe all the glories of the gospel. Even John said the whole "world itself could not contain the books that should be written" (John 21:25) if all the teachings and beauty of the Savior's life and gospel were recorded. I am afraid I do not have the ability to write about even one aspect of the gospel, let alone that which is described as the most glorious. I have hesitated for a long time to attempt to speak or write about the temple. Perhaps others whose powers and gifts are far greater than mine would still not be able to do sufficient justice to so wonderful a topic, but my deep interest in the temple has urged me to make the attempt, perhaps only for my own clarification and edification. I hoped, as I commenced, that the Lord surely would not withhold his blessing on the labors of one who loved his subject so freely.

Regardless of the outcome, the labor itself has brought me many returns. I have often felt as Frederic Farrar did while attempting to write *The Life of Christ.* He too felt overwhelmed by his topic. In his preface he writes: "Whether this book be . . . blessed to high ends, or whether it be received with harshness and indifference, nothing at least can rob me of the deep and constant happiness which I have felt during almost every hour that has been spent upon it. . . . Even in the midst of incessant labor at other things, nothing forbade that the subject on which I was engaged should be often in my thoughts, or that I should find in it a source of peace and happiness different, alike in kind and in degree, from any which other interests could either give or take away." (*The Life of Christ,* p. 2.)

PART 1

THE GREAT SYMBOL OF OUR MEMBERSHIP

O Lord, we regard with intense and indescribable feelings the completion of this sacred house.

(SALT LAKE TEMPLE DEDICATORY PRAYER.)

CHAPTER 1

How High a Priority?

While I was teaching at BYU, I had the opportunity to participate in the inauguration of President Rex E. Lee. It was a wonderful occasion. On Friday morning the faculty, dressed in the robes of academia, waited in the parking lot for the processional to begin. At a given signal we all marched into the Marriott Center and took our seats. Thousands of students entered, and soon the auditorium was filled. All were excited, and the atmosphere of the Marriott Center was one of general anticipation.

Numerous dignitaries from the state and community arrived, taking their seats of honor. Finally a number of the General Authorities, including members of the First Presidency, arrived with President Lee. They took their seats on the stand, and the meeting began. It was truly an exciting and important event, and I felt privileged to be part of it.

As the ceremonies continued, I realized that among all the dignitaries and officials, President Ezra Taft Benson was not in attendance. I wondered if his health was failing and, therefore, he could not attend. I had heard him speak recently, and he had seemed vigorous and strong. Were there other meetings or duties he needed to attend to as he carried the weight of his prophetic mantle?

The inauguration lasted several hours. It was interesting and edifying, but I took home a tiny, nagging thought: Where was President Benson?

The next Friday, I attended a special ward endowment session in the Jordan River Temple. Before participating in the ordinances, we had the opportunity to listen to a member of the temple presidency. In his remarks I found an answer to my puzzlement of the week before. As well as I can remember, this is what he told us: "Every Friday morning, President and Sister Benson come to the Jordan River Temple to participate in an endowment session. We meet them at a private door and help them prepare for their session. Last Friday we assumed they would not attend the temple as they normally do because of the inauguration of President Lee at Brigham Young University.

"To our surprise they arrived at their usual hour, and we were not prepared to greet them and offer our customary assistance. We apologized, telling President Benson we enjoyed greeting them and helping them but had thought they would be at BYU. President Benson smiled and asked: 'What day is it?' 'Friday,' we answered. Then he replied 'Friday is my temple day. Where else would I be on a Friday morning?'"

As I listened to this tiny but wonderful story from the life of the president of the Church, I couldn't help but marvel at the power of his example. To the inauguration of the president of a great university, an event that takes place maybe once every ten years, President Benson could send a counselor. He, himself, would attend an ordinary endowment session in the Jordan River Temple as was his custom. That morning he chose to wear the sacred clothing of the temple rather than the honored robes of academia.

I realize that other factors could have entered into his decision to be in the temple that Friday morning. Other demands may have led to his choice. But I couldn't help but be impressed with his decision, and since that day the importance of attending the temple has been magnified in my eyes.

How high in our priorities have we placed the temple? Have we placed it as high as President Benson and other prophets who preceded him? He is not alone in his emphasis on the importance of the work that takes place in the House of the Lord. Holy men have so testified through the ages, and particularly during this last dispensation, for "it is in strict accordance with the divine will that the great work for the salvation of the dead was one assigned to those who lived in the dispensation of the fullness of times." (Joseph Fielding Smith, in *Improve-*

ment Era, April 1966, p. 273.) Let us review the emphasis placed on this edifying work by past prophets.

THE GREAT HYMN OF THE RESTORATION

In September 1842, the Prophet Joseph Smith was hiding in the house of Edward Hunter in Nauvoo. His enemies were after him again. He had been tormented and persecuted for so many years that he could write: "As for the perils which I am called to pass through, they seem but a small thing to me, as the envy and wrath of man have been my common lot all the days of my life." (D&C 127:2.) Yet it was in the cramped quarters of Edward Hunter's home that Joseph penned the most majestic hymn of praise of the Restoration.

Perhaps you have been to a symphony and listened to a piece of music that begins with a single, clear note played by a violin or a flute. The single instrument holds center stage for a time and then slowly, sometimes almost imperceptibly, is joined by other instruments. As the piece continues, the music swells as more and more instruments join in until all are playing and the whole hall is filled with the beauty of sound.

Or perhaps you have listened to a great choir perform. Often a single soloist with a clear voice will begin to sing. As with the symphony, that single voice sounds in our ears without distraction. Then, slowly, other voices begin singing until, in a wonderful unity of sound, all are singing as one.

This is the structure of Joseph Smith's hymn of praise, only it is a hymn not of voice in song or note of violin but in words played upon the soul and recorded in the scriptures. Joseph's hymn, too, begins with a single voice, "a voice of gladness." Listen to the words and see if you can hear the other voices join in to sing one unified song of praise for the blessings of the Restoration:

"Now what do we hear in the gospel which we have received? A voice of gladness! A voice of mercy from heaven; and a voice of truth out of the earth; glad tidings for the dead; a voice of gladness for the living and the dead; glad tidings of great joy. . . .

"And again, what do we hear? Glad tidings from Cumorah! Moroni, an angel from heaven, declaring the fulfilment of the prophets. . . . A voice of the Lord in the wilderness of Fayette. . . . The voice of Michael on the banks of the Susquehanna. . . . The voice of Peter, James, and John in the wilderness. . . .

"And again, the voice of God in the chamber of old Father Whitmer. . . . And the voice of Michael, the archangel; the voice of Gabriel, and of Raphael, and of divers angels, from Michael or Adam down to the present time, all declaring their dispensation, their rights, their keys, their honors, their majesty and glory, and the power of their priesthood . . . confirming our hope! . . .

"Let the earth break forth into singing. Let the dead speak forth anthems of eternal praise to the King Immanuel, who hath ordained, before the world was, that which would enable us to redeem them out of their prison. . . .

"Let the mountains shout for joy, and all ye valleys cry aloud; and all ye seas and dry lands tell the wonders of your Eternal King! And ye rivers, and brooks, and rills, flow down with gladness. Let the woods and all the trees of the field praise the Lord; and ye solid rocks weep for joy! And let the sun, moon, and the morning stars sing together, and let all the sons of God shout for joy! And let the eternal creations declare his name forever and ever! And again I say, how glorious is the voice we hear from heaven, proclaiming in our ears, glory, and salvation, and honor, and immortality, and eternal life; kingdoms, principalities, and powers!" (D&C 128:19–23.)

What could have possibly been on Joseph Smith's mind to bring forth from his pen such a beautiful summation of the Restoration? The central theme of section 128 is the salvation of the dead through the ordinances of the House of the Lord. Indeed, the verse immediately preceding Joseph's song of gladness speaks of a "welding link . . . between the fathers and the children," a link that would be "whole and complete and perfect." (D&C 128:18.)

Earlier in the letter, and serving as introduction to his song of praise, Joseph Smith told the Saints, "[The work of the temple] seems to occupy my mind, and press itself upon my feelings the strongest." He assured them, "These are principles in relation to the dead and the living that cannot be lightly passed over, as pertaining to our salvation." (D&C 128:1, 15.) Joseph understood that the culmination of the

Restoration, the point to which all the voices were leading, was the temple and the redeeming work for both living and dead that would take place within its walls. Without that work, the song of the Restoration would have "become as sounding brass, or a tinkling cymbal." (1 Corinthians 13:1.) Or, as Malachi wrote, "The whole earth would be utterly wasted at his coming." (D&C 2:3.) Temple work was the soul of Joseph Smith's song as it is the soul of the Restoration.

THE KEYSTONE OF THE GOSPEL ARCH

Many other prophets have added their own testimony to that of Joseph Smith. Wilford Woodruff told the Saints that Joseph's "soul was wound up with this work [temple work] before he was martyred for the word of God and testimony of Jesus Christ. He told us that there must be a welding link of all dispensations and of the work of God from one generation to another. This was upon his mind *more than most any other subject that was given to him." (Discourses of Wilford Woodruff*, p. 156; emphasis added.)

President Woodruff then added his own testimony: "Ye sons of men, I say unto you, in the name of Israel's God, those very principles that God has revealed are what have stayed the judgments of the Almighty on the earth. *Were it not for these principles, you and I would not be here today.* (Ibid., p. 154; emphasis added.)

Elder Boyd K. Packer said, "It is evident that the work relating to temples bothers the adversary the most." (*The Holy Temple*, p. 216.) It is this work that causes all "the bells of hell [to begin] to ring," as Brigham Young stated. (*Discourses of Brigham Young*, p. 628.)

John A. Widtsoe called temple work "the *keystone of the wonderful Gospel arch.* If this center stone is weakened, and falls out, the whole arch falls into a heap of unorganized doctrinal blocks. It is a high privilege for young or old to be allowed to enter the House of the Lord, there to serve God and to win power." ("Temple Worship," p. 64; emphasis added.) In light of this perspective, is it any wonder "the devils in hell . . . [are] trying to overthrow" the Saints and stop the work? (*Discourses of Brigham Young*, p. 618.)

Heber J. Grant, who, like President Benson, found "the time to go to the temple and do temple work once a week" (*Gospel Standards,*

p. 257) told the Saints of his day, "If you get it into your heart and soul that this is one of the *most important things* you as Latter-day Saints can do, you will find a way to do it." (*Improvement Era*, 44:459; emphasis added.) Joseph Fielding Smith called temple work the "*greatest and grandest duty* of all" and encouraged the Saints not to neglect "the *weightier privilege* and commandment, notwithstanding all other good works." (*Seeking After Our Dead*, p. 36; emphasis added.)

President Brigham Young said temple work "is to be the greatest work man ever performed on the earth." (*Discourses of Brigham Young*, p. 623.) President Spencer W. Kimball said temple work is "a grave responsibility that we cannot avoid," one that would place us "in jeopardy if we fail to do this important work." (*Ensign*, January 1977, p. 5.)

Perhaps King David best described the desired attitude toward the temple in the psalms. It is an attitude based on love of the temple, not a duty or responsibility placed upon his shoulders. The sweetness of David's words are an example to us all. "One thing have I desired of the Lord," David sang, "that will I seek after; that I may dwell in the house of the Lord all the days of my life, to behold the beauty of the Lord, and to enquire in his temple." (Psalm 27:4.) In a later psalm he wrote, "I was glad when they said unto me, Let us go into the house of the Lord." (Psalm 122:1.) David's soul, with that of all the prophets, "longeth, yea, even fainteth for the courts of the Lord," for those courts are "amiable." (Psalm 84:1–2.) Should not all of our souls also long for them?

In light of this emphasis, it is not hard to understand why the prophet of the Lord chose to be in the temple on a Friday morning instead of in the Marriott Center for the inauguration of a new university president. It is not difficult to comprehend the hymn of praise Joseph Smith wrote while hiding in the cramped quarters of Bishop Hunter's house. Nor does it take great thought to see why President Howard W. Hunter issued an invitation at his first press conference (and reemphasized it in his first General Conference address) to all the Saints to "establish the temple of the Lord as *the great symbol of their membership* and the supernal setting for their most sacred covenants." He continued: "It would be the *deepest desire* of my heart to have every member of the Church temple worthy. . . . Let us be a . . . temple-loving people." (*Church News*, June 11, 1994, p. 14; emphasis added.)

PART 2

HOUSE OF LEARNING

Today we dedicate the whole unto Thee, with all that pertains unto it that it may be holy in Thy sight; that it may be a house of prayer, a house of praise and of worship; that Thy glory may rest upon it; that Thy holy presence may be continually in it; that it may be the abode of Thy Well-Beloved Son, our Savior; that the angels who stand before Thy face may be the hallowed messengers who shall visit it, bearing to us Thy wishes and Thy will, that it may be sanctified and consecrated in all its parts holy unto Thee, the God of Israel, the Almighty Ruler of mankind.

(SALT LAKE TEMPLE DEDICATORY PRAYER.)

CHAPTER 2

Learning to Learn from Symbols

Most of us have a vivid memory of the first time we went to the temple to receive our endowments. I was a newly called missionary and had traveled to the Los Angeles Temple. I did not know what to expect. Although some aspects of my own endowment were wonderfully edifying to me, much of it was confusing. I left bewildered and a little frightened. I have since discovered that my experience was not unique. I have also discovered why my first experience was not all I had anticipated. I did not understand the manner in which the Lord teaches his children in his house. Had I understood, my anxiety and confusion would have disappeared, even though my comprehension level might have remained the same.

ENDOWED WITH POWER

The Doctrine and Covenants teaches us that in the temple we will be "endowed with power from on high." (D&C 38:32.) Much of that power comes from the knowledge or intelligence we receive. Therefore, to be endowed with the power the Lord wishes us to receive, we must learn how to learn in his house.

In the temple the Spirit is the teacher. It instructs us, most frequently, through the symbols that comprise the endowment. We must be alert and pay attention to all that we see and hear, thus allowing the Spirit to teach us and to bring us understanding. If we go to the temple and just sit, without making an effort to learn, we will miss most of the greatest blessings the temple has to offer. "When you return [to the

11

temple]," Elder David B. Haight taught, "come with an open, seeking, contrite heart, and allow the Spirit to teach you by revelation *what the symbols can mean to you.*" (*Conference Report,* April 1992, p. 20; emphasis added.) The true teaching in the temple is not group instruction. Each soul is invited to have his or her own personal tutor, that of the Spirit, who will tailor the symbols to specific needs and levels of maturity while inviting the active participation of each individual in the learning process. This type of teaching led Elder John A. Widtsoe to remark: "I wish instruction were given so well in every school room throughout the land, for we would then teach with more effect than we now do." ("Temple Worship.")

In the dedicatory prayer of the Kirtland Temple, Joseph Smith prayed that all who came to the temple might "grow up in thee, and receive a fulness of the Holy Ghost." (D&C 109:15.) This "fulness" is essential in uncovering the depths the temple ordinances reveal. Since worthiness and purity of life qualify us to receive the gifts and companionship of the Holy Ghost, the covenants and lifestyle taught in the temple, which we bind ourselves to live, in and of themselves bring the fulness promised in Joseph Smith's prayer. In addition, the serenity and peace of the temple itself also contribute to the fulness of the Holy Ghost. In the temple, our spirits are more calm, and we are removed from the noise and turmoil of the outside world, giving the Spirit more of a chance to whisper truth to our souls. With the fulness of the Holy Ghost, we can be taught on a much higher level.

Joseph Smith once instructed the Saints on the increasing power of the Spirit to reveal truth to our minds. He said: "A person may profit by noticing the first intimation of the spirit of revelation; for instance, when you feel pure intelligence flowing into you, it may give you sudden strokes of ideas. . . . Thus by *learning* the Spirit of God and understanding it, you may *grow into the principle of revelation,* until you become perfect in Christ Jesus." (*Teachings of the Prophet Joseph Smith,* p. 151; emphasis added.) Notice that we *learn* and *grow* into the principle of revelation. We may not receive a fulness at first, but it will come as we continue to seek understanding in the temple. Remember, we are also invited to "grow up" in the Lord's house. As our own spirits mature, we are more receptive to the teachings of the Holy Ghost.

This maturity cannot reach its fulness without the temple. In truth, the very word *endowment* suggests a gift that brings gradual yet continual growth.

An endowment is a gift, but it is a special kind of gift. Most secular endowments are established to be self-perpetuating. For instance, a company gives an endowment of a large sum of money to a university to fund the arts or medical research. The university does not spend the original gift. They are allowed to spend only the interest that the original gift generates. The temple endowment was designed in a similar fashion. Its symbolic nature allows it to teach or give continually through many years of a person's life. Jesus promised the woman at the well, "The water that I shall give . . . shall be . . . a well of water springing up into everlasting life." (John 4:14.) It would continue to pour forth its sweetness constantly. The endowment's power is its ability to send into our minds and hearts knowledge in an uninterrupted flow. The symbols are the original gift of the endowment. The multiplicity of meaning and edification are the self-perpetuating interest the original gift generates.

"VAST REALITIES"

Elder John A. Widtsoe explained, "The endowment itself is symbolic; it is a series of symbols of vast realities, too vast for full understanding. Those who go through the temple and come out feeling that the service is unbeautiful have been so occupied with the outward form as to fail to understand the inner meaning. It is the meaning of things that counts in life. . . .

"Temple worship implies a *great effort of mind and concentration* if we are to understand the mighty symbols that pass in review before us. Everything must be arranged to attune our hearts, our minds, and our souls to the work. . . .

"To the man or woman who goes through the temple, with *open eyes, heeding the symbols* and the covenants, and making a *steady, continuous effort* to understand the full meaning, God speaks his word, and revelations come. The endowment is so richly symbolic. . . . It is so packed full of revelations to those who exercise their strength to seek and see, that no human words can explain or make clear the possibilities that reside in the temple service. The endowment which was given by revelation can best be understood by revelation; and to those who seek most vigorously, with pure hearts, will the revelation be greatest." ("Temple Worship," p. 63.) It is this rich depth of symbolism that makes the endowment an inexhaustible source of knowledge and edification.

On occasion I have been asked, "Why are the symbols of the temple so different from anything we have experienced in the Church before?" They are different for a wonderful purpose that shows the great wisdom of the Lord. The different nature of the symbols itself demands explanation. It almost forces us to ask questions. It invites pondering and reflection. We find ourselves naturally asking: "What does that mean? Why do we do that? Why are we shown this? What is the meaning of the clothing?" Perhaps that is what the Lord wants us to do, and to keep doing it until answers come. The symbols are different so we will not become so accustomed to seeing them that we cease asking the questions. If you are puzzled by the symbols of the temple, perhaps that is as it should be. It is all right to keep on puzzling over them and pondering them and studying them, allowing the Spirit to reveal their power one by one. The danger is not that we think them unusual but that we stop thinking. The symbols stand out to help us overcome this human tendency.

It is also important to remember that the temple ordinances constitute a whole. They are like a four-act play, a beautiful poem with four stanzas, or a song with four verses. We may have a favorite act or stanza or verse, but to receive the full meaning of the work, we must remain aware of all four acts, stanzas, or verses. Let us return to the baptistry, frequently perform the initiatory ordinances, and participate in sealings. We will learn more if we do this than if we constantly repeat only the the endowment session.

THE POWER OF SYMBOLIC LANGUAGE

Teaching through symbols can be very powerful. Symbols can suggest many different truths to different people at different times in their lives. Thus they edify us according to our present needs and never become irrelevant.

The power of symbolic writing was wonderfully explained by George MacDonald, a mentor of Christian apologist C. S. Lewis. Although he was not speaking of temple symbolism, his insight is applicable. "A genuine work of art must mean many things," he wrote. "The truer its art, *the more things it will mean.*" There is no truer artist than the Lord, and, of course, his masterpiece is found in the holy temple. If mortal symbols can mean many things, how much more can we expect to discover in the symbols presented by the Lord?

MacDonald continued his description of the power of symbolic language with these thoughts: "The *best thing* you can do for your fellow, next to rousing his conscience, is—not to give him things to think about, but to *wake things up* that are in him; or say, to *make him think things for himself.*

"The best Nature does for us is to work in us such moods in which *thoughts of high import arise.* Does any aspect of Nature wake but one thought? Does she ever suggest only one definite thing? Does she make any two men in the same place at the same moment think the same thing? Is she therefore a failure, because she is not definite? Is it nothing that she rouses the something deeper than the understanding—the power that underlies thoughts? . . . Nature is *mood-engendering, thought-provoking.* . . .

"In everything that God has made, there is layer upon layer of ascending significance; also he expresses the same thought in higher and higher kinds of that thought. . . .

"If a writer's aim be logical conviction, he must spare no logical pains, not merely to be understood, but to escape being misunderstood; where his object is to *move by suggestion, to cause to imagine,* then let him assail the soul of his reader as the wind assails an aeolian harp. If there be music in my reader, I would gladly wake it." (*The Gifts of the Child Christ* 1:23–28; emphasis added.)

MacDonald's insights are especially true of the temple. Generally speaking, we do not "learn" the meanings of the great, exalting symbols of the gospel. Rather we "remember" their meanings, for we were taught the power that lies behind them before our births. On earth, a veil has been drawn across our minds, but we are frequently reminded that the veil is thin in the Lord's house. The word *awakening* is a good description of how knowledge is often imparted in the Lord's house. Remember, the Holy Ghost is the teacher in the temple, and we are promised we can receive a fulness of his power. Jesus taught his disciples at the Last Supper that one of the missions of the Holy Ghost is to "bring all things to [our] remembrance." (John 14:26.)

President Joseph F. Smith also suggested this awakening to truths through the power of the Spirit: "All those salient truths which come home so forcibly to the head and heart seem but the *awakening of the memories of the spirit. Can we know anything here that we did not know before we came?* Are not the means of knowledge in the first estate equal to those of this?" But in order to tap into that knowledge we must struggle to get past "the prison-house of mortality." (*Gospel Doctrine,* p. 13; emphasis added.)

Hope and confidence are engendered in this truth. Our task of discovery in the temple appears more likely of success if we realize that the myriad truths found there are sleeping in our memories already. We must call upon the Spirit to help us awaken them.

Those who attend the temple frequently and are familiar with the Lord's way of teaching have already discovered that a meaning behind a symbol tends to come "all at once," as a remembered or awakened truth, or not at all. Or, as Joseph Smith said, "A person may profit by noticing the first intimation of the spirit of revelation; for instance, when you feel *pure intelligence* flowing into you, it may give you *sudden strokes of ideas.*" (*Teachings of the Prophet Joseph Smith,* p. 151; emphasis added.)

C. S. Lewis, commenting on George MacDonald's understanding of symbolic writing, added insights from his own experience: "It goes beyond the expression of things we have already felt. It arouses in us sensations we have never had before, never anticipated having, as though we had broken out of our normal mode of consciousness and 'possessed joys not promised to our birth'. It gets under our skin, hits us at a level deeper than our thoughts or even our passions, troubles oldest certainties till all questions are re-opened, and in general shocks us more fully awake than we are for most of our lives." (George MacDonald, *An Anthology,* pp. 16–17.)

Though MacDonald's and Lewis's descriptions were written about literary works, they describe the essence of the temple mode of instruction. We must learn how to learn in the Lord's way. In his house that method is largely symbolic, because symbols provide one of the most all-encompassing and powerful ways to learn. We must learn to trust the power inherent in symbols, even though we may feel ourselves children in their deciphering. With time and patience, our spirits will mature, the fulness of the Holy Ghost will distill upon us, and the awakening will begin.

The truths of the temple are profoundly beautiful, edifying, and joyful. Our own desire and effort to discover them must be equal to that beauty if their full force and wonder is to be truly appreciated. Thus the Lord protects the sacredness of his deepest and most holy truths, presenting them only to those who most deeply desire them and whose lives of sacrifice and obedience have developed in them a closeness with the Spirit. Much is also accomplished outside the temple. The more our lives reflect the obedience and dedication the Lord desires, the more powerfully the Spirit operates within us. When we take this increased power of the Spirit into the temple, we can expect to be taught wonderful and edifying truths to bless our lives and those of our families.

CHAPTER 3

Preliminary Lessons

The Lord does not leave us without help as we learn how to learn in his house. He prepares us in a number of ways. Some of these preparations begin early in our childhood. Others come as we enter his temple and participate in the ordinances. All of them continue throughout our lives.

SYMBOLIC ORDINANCES

Before we even go to the temple, we are introduced to symbolic ordinances. Through them we are shown how to respond to symbolic language. The sacrament and baptism are such ordinances. If those unfamiliar with LDS or Christian worship entered an LDS chapel and witnessed the sacrament or a baptism, it might appear strange to them. Unless they understood what the outward actions and objects represented, they might even be repelled by what they saw.

In the sacrament, the bread reminds us of the body of the Savior, and the water of his blood. When we partake, we think of his loving sacrifice in our behalf and of our covenants that make his sacrifice efficacious in our lives. The bread and water can also remind us that Jesus was "the bread of life" and that he is the source of "living water." (See John 6.) Our focus, therefore, is centered on the meaning of the symbol and not on the symbol itself. When we understand the meanings of temple symbols, their outward forms become beautiful, just as the sacrament is beautiful and edifying to us.

Baptism is an excellent ordinance to study to give us a better idea of how the Lord teaches in the temple. What does baptism symbolize? Some may say baptism is symbolic of a cleansing. The font reminds us of a bath where our sins are washed away. As we are immersed in the water, we become pure. This is taught in the scriptures.

Others may teach that baptism symbolizes a birth. The font represents the womb. As a newborn baby emerges from the water of the mother's womb, so too are we "born again" through the waters of baptism into a new and innocent life. This also is affirmed in the scriptures.

Others might add that baptism is a symbolic burial. The font suggests to the mind a grave. The old man of sin, the natural man, is buried in the water so that a new man of Christ may be resurrected. This we do in similitude of the Savior's death and resurrection. This interpretation is also suggested in the scriptures.

Is baptism a bath, a birth, or a burial? It is all of them. Because such symbols convey multiple meanings, they will, if we continue to ponder them, constantly edify and instruct us throughout our lives.

A MANUAL FOR THE ENDOWMENT

Just as we have considered the meanings of the sacrament and of baptism, so we must learn to do with all the ordinances of the Lord's house. The Lord has shown us a pattern in the sacrament and in baptism, but we do not need to uncover the layers of symbolic meaning without assistance. Help is available. All three of the above meanings of baptism are taught in the scriptures, as are the multiple meanings of the sacrament.

Occasionally I have been asked if I can recommend a good book or article to help people understand the temple ordinances. I have always answered, "Yes! There is a wonderful manual written to explain even the most subtle meanings of the endowment, and it is readily available to you." Excitedly the person takes out pencil and paper to write down the title. "The manual is the holy scriptures," I say. Disappointed, the person puts down the pencil and says, "No, really. Is there any other book you would recommend?"

What good is it to read anything else about the temple (including this present volume) if we have not studied deeply the greatest source

of information available? Surely the prominent placement of the scriptures in the temple is a hint to us of their value in comprehending all
that we see and hear within its walls. The scriptures will reveal deeper
and broader meanings about the temple. Within their pages are the
keys to much of the temple symbolism. Every time we are told to "seek
. . . diligently . . . words of wisdom . . . out of the best books" (D&C
88:118), it is in the context of temple worship. The Lord is suggesting
that insights to temple truths lie in a fuller and more intense study of
the scriptures. The more we know the scriptures, the more the endowment will open to our understanding. Many have had the experience
of pondering in the temple when a verse of scripture arises in the mind
and insight about the "vast realities" is received.

The temple endowment is scripture, the highest form of scripture,
not written down for all to read and see but engraved in the minds of
those whose efforts and attendance show the depth of their desires. It
is written on our hearts, not in the pages of a book. Occasionally we
read of people who are shown truths or are taught principles they are
forbidden to reveal or write down. Jesus prayed with the Nephites, for
example, and "the things which he prayed cannot be written." (3 Nephi
17:15.) The moment was sacred, too holy and profoundly beautiful to
commit to paper.

As an English major, I used to wish I could see or hear something
so wonderful it could not be written. Then, one day, the Spirit whispered, "You have, many times, in the Lord's house." The endowment
and other temple ordinances are too sacred to be written down for all
to see. The Lord told Mormon when he was about to include more of
the Savior's words in the Book of Mormon, "I will try the faith of my
people." (3 Nephi 26:11.) So, too, the Lord tries the faith of his people
before they receive the sacred truths and covenants of his house.

Since the endowment is scripture, and since scripture is the best
commentary on other scripture, in our reading of the Standard Works
we should expect to find insight about the endowment. This will occur
especially if we remember that symbols can have multiple meanings.
Perhaps an illustration of how scripture comments on scripture will
help to clarify this point.

RUN AND NOT BE WEARY, WALK AND NOT FAINT

For many years I read the promises attached to the Word of Wisdom as they are recorded in section 89 of the Doctrine and Covenants. One of those promises indicates that we will "run and not be weary, and . . . walk and not faint." (V. 20.) For many years I thought I understood fully the meaning of this promise. It was an assurance of a healthy body if the counsel in the Word of Wisdom was followed. I still believe this is true and inherent in the promise.

However, one day I was reading Paul's epistle to the Hebrews and saw in his words a deeper and to me more powerful promise. Paul frequently used the image of an Olympic race to describe life to the early Saints. "Let us lay aside every weight," he wrote, "and the sin which doth so easily beset us, and let us *run with patience the race* that is set before us, looking unto Jesus the author and finisher of our faith; who for the joy that was set before him endured the cross, despising the shame, and is set down at the right hand of the throne of God. For consider him that endured such contradiction of sinners against himself, lest ye be *wearied and faint* in your minds." (Hebrews 12:1–3; emphasis added.)

Three words from the promise in section 89 are also in Paul's encouraging words to the early Saints: "run," "weary," and "faint." But in Hebrews, the race is spiritual, not physical. Other scriptures then come to mind. We are frequently told in the scriptures not to be "weary of well doing" and to walk the "strait and narrow path."

If we put all these ideas together, a deeper meaning to the promise arises. The promise in the Word of Wisdom is also an assurance of spiritual endurance. We will run the race of life and not be weary in well doing, and we will walk the strait and narrow path and not faint. In other words, we will "endure to the end."

What we have done here with the Word of Wisdom can be done with the phrases, covenants, and promises we hear and see in the temple. New and wonderful insights will be laid at our feet if we are willing to pay the price by *seeking* "learning, even by study [of the scriptures] and also by faith." (D&C 88:118.)

Scriptural Practice with Symbols

The importance of scripture study as it relates to the temple is also seen in the fact that the scriptures themselves are symbolic and contain many layers of meaning. When my children have taken college entrance examinations like the ACT or the SAT, they have studied books that contain the kinds of questions they will encounter in the real tests. That allows them to practice taking the test and be better prepared.

We can also view the scriptures that way—as practice symbols, language, and ordinances. An excellent example is the book of Exodus. In a way, it is a Mosaic endowment. It is a small microcosm of life, just as the endowment is a microcosm of life. Almost everything that happens in it, from the freeing of the children of Israel to their entry into the promised land, can be symbolically applied to our own lives.

For example, let us study the pillar of fire or cloud that guided the Israelites as they traveled through the wilderness. Paul tells us that the crossing of the Red Sea was a symbolic baptism for Israel. After baptism, we are given the gift of the Holy Ghost, who serves as a guide throughout our lives. This gift remains with us as long as we are worthy.

The pillar of fire or cloud in Exodus suggests to our minds the Holy Ghost, who will guide us just as the pillar guided the Israelites across the wilderness. The wilderness suggests life on earth, and the promised land suggests the celestial kingdom. With this in mind, notice the powerful symbolic lesson this story teaches us. The attitude the children of Israel have toward the pillar of fire should also be our attitude toward the guidance of the Holy Ghost: "So it was alway: the cloud covered it by day, and the appearance of fire by night. And when the cloud was taken up from the tabernacle, then after that the children of Israel journeyed: and in the place where the cloud abode, there the children of Israel pitched their tents. At the commandment of the Lord the children of Israel journeyed, and at the commandment of the Lord they pitched: as long as the cloud abode upon the tabernacle they rested in their tents. And when the cloud tarried long upon the tabernacle many days then the children of Israel kept the charge of the Lord, and journeyed not. And so it was, when the cloud was a few days upon the tabernacle . . . they abode in their tents. . . . And so it was, when the cloud abode from even unto the morning, and that the cloud was taken up in the morning, then they journeyed: whether it was by day or by night that the cloud was taken up, they journeyed. Or whether it were two days, or a month, or a year, that the cloud tarried upon the tabernacle, remaining thereon, the children of Israel abode in their tents, . . . but when it was taken up, they journeyed. At the commandment of the Lord they rested . . . and at the commandment of the Lord they journeyed." (Numbers 9:16–23.)

What a marvelous lesson is suggested by this story if we understand the symbolism of the pillar that rested over the tabernacle. In our own lives, we must never journey without the direction of the Spirit. We must stay with the Spirit no matter when, where, or how long it journeys or rests. It controls the direction of our lives. Sometimes in the day the pillar would move, and sometimes at night. It didn't matter how long the people had camped, be it two days or a year. The pillar determined everything. Their desire was always to be where the pillar wanted them to be.

Other wonderful messages are contained in the story of the children of Israel. For example, they were instructed to gather the manna everyday. Moses tells us in Deuteronomy that the manna symbolized the word of God. (See Deuteronomy 8:3.) Should we not gather the words of God from the scriptures "every day?" Can we gather enough on one day to last the week? Do we not gather a little here and a little there until we have enough to satisfy our spiritual hunger? Work was necessary in gathering enough manna to feed one's family. Is not effort also required to gather from the scriptures and words of the prophets the wisdom to feed our modern families the "bread of life"? Jesus, referring to this story, called himself the "bread of life" in the sixth chapter of John. Here also we see multiple meanings in the richness of the scripture narrative. He also was the bread "which cometh down from heaven." (John 6:33.)

Israel followed Moses through the wilderness. Do we not follow living prophets through the wilderness of modern life? He led them to Sinai, the mountain of the Lord, where they were to "meet with God," hear his voice, and receive his law. Is not our own prophet, Gordon B.

Hinckley, seeking with all his heart to lead us to the mountain of the Lord's house, the Sinai of the temple, where we also meet with God, hear his voice, and receive his law? During their wanderings in the wilderness, Israel frequently desired to return to the "fleshpots" of Egypt. Egypt suggests the captivity and restraining power of the world and the adversary. Do we not also struggle to remain separate from the world, to feast continually on the manna of the Lord's word and not the "fleshpots" of worldly entertainments and appetites?

These and other stories teach us in a manner similar to the way the temple narrative instructs. We must learn to see ourselves in the images and story that are portrayed before us. A constant reading of the scriptures will give us practice in this method of instruction, particularly the stories and narratives of the Old Testament. In time we will become proficient, and the temple will begin to open up and weigh significantly on our everyday choices and activities.

We cannot speak outside the temple of the symbols or the narrative portrayed in the endowment, but we can discuss the story of the children of Israel and other scriptural stories all we like. We can help each other learn how to find personal relevance in the story of another person or people. In short, we can practice temple learning and help each other begin to see beyond the symbols to the vast realities they represent.

SIMPLE AND OBVIOUS SYMBOLS

The Lord helps us learn how to learn from the temple in other ways. He has deliberately made some of the temple symbols easy to understand. Some of these symbols have also been explained to us by the living prophets and apostles. For example, in the temple everyone wears white clothing, which symbolizes purity and cleanliness in the sight of God and each other. It has also been explained that it suggests an equality in the sight of God that creates unity and oneness in his children. Could it also teach that as white is a reflection of all the beautiful colors of the spectrum, so too our lives must reflect all the multifaceted beauty of the Savior's gospel light?

The reflecting mirrors that face each other in different rooms of the temple suggest to us eternity. This symbol is easy to understand if we take time to ponder. It is truly an appropriate symbol in the sealing rooms, for there eternal families are created and an eternal journey as husband and wife is commenced. The Lord designed the temple ordinances so that all of us can understand some of the symbols. This helps us avoid discouragement until we learn to unveil the deeper symbols with their multiple possibilities to edify and instruct.

DEEPER SYMBOLS

Some symbols of the temple are more difficult to understand, so we are given a meaning when they are presented to us. In some cases we are given multiple meanings. If we ponder the given explanation of the symbol and how it relates to the symbol itself, we will become more familiar with the Lord's teaching method. These symbols we hold sacred and do not speak of outside temple walls—not because we are secretive but because we reverence them too highly to allow them to become trivial in common conversation, open to anyone who is curious.

After presenting us with symbolic ordinances before we ever go to the temple, after giving us symbolic images and language in the scriptures, after presenting us with some easier symbols to understand, and after explaining the meaning of others that are more difficult, the Lord in essence says to us: "Do you now comprehend how I teach in my house? I have tried to prepare you for temple worship for a lifetime. Now that you have an idea of how I teach, spend the rest of your life frequently returning to learn all that my house can teach you. Ponder and pray until you understand the symbols I have not explained. Let every word, every act, and all you see be an opportunity for insight and edification." If we approach temple worship this way, every visit is an invitation for discovery. It requires effort and concentration, but the Lord assures us we will not be disappointed.

EVERYTHING CAN TEACH

We should also realize that everything in the temple can teach us. The words, the covenants, the clothing, and the architecture all present opportunities for wonderful insight. I once learned a great lesson on marriage while witnessing the sealing of a relative. After the ceremony,

I stood with my wife looking into the mirrors that reflect a strait and narrow path into eternity. As usual, I was moving this way and that way, trying to see a little farther, but my own reflection was in the way, and I could not see as far as I wanted. I remember consciously thinking: "I wish I could take myself out of the mirrors. I could see eternity better, but I keep getting in the way."

As I pondered this, the Spirit bore a strong witness to its truth. Concentrating too much on ourselves obscures our view of eternal things. I thought of all the couples I had counseled while serving as bishop and realized that in every case of marital conflict, one or both partners had focused so much on themselves that they could no longer see eternity. I wanted to bring each couple in my ward to the sealing room, stand them in front of the mirrors, and say: "Can you see what we sometimes do? Can you understand the problem and also perceive the solution? The mirrors teach us a powerful truth that can strengthen, enhance, or save our marriages."

My eyes rested on the chandelier that hung above the altar. It cast a soft and gentle light in the room and suggested to me the light that radiates from the Holy Spirit. I pondered all the other words from the scriptures that are associated with light, such as truth, spirit, intelligence, the Savior, and so on. I watched the chandelier's reflection multiply down the corridor created by the mirrors, and the Spirit seemed to whisper: "If you want your marriage to be eternal, you must take the Spirit, the truth, and the Savior with you. This light will guide you through the corridors of time and into eternity."

Perhaps this beautiful truth is suggested by President Wilford Woodruff in the dedicatory prayer he offered for the Salt Lake Temple: "Our Father in heaven, we present before Thee the altars which we have prepared for Thy servants and handmaidens to receive their sealing blessings. We dedicate them in the name of the Lord Jesus Christ, unto Thy most holy name, and we ask Thee to sanctify these altars, that those who come unto them *may feel the power of the Holy Ghost resting upon them.*" (*Temples of the Most High*, p. 125; emphasis added.)

These simple truths, among others, were taught to me by the furnishings of the sealing room alone. How much more can we learn when we consider the power of the ordinances themselves and the rich detail of their language? We must constantly ask ourselves each time we go to the temple: "What can this teach me? What can I learn from this part of the ordinance? How are these words and these images relevant to my life? Why is the Lord showing me this? Why does the Lord ask me to do this?"

Most of all, we must not become discouraged. It was never intended that we understand the temple ordinances all at once. They were designed to feed us for a lifetime. Joseph Smith once said, "The endowment you are so anxious about, you cannot comprehend now, nor could Gabriel explain it to the understanding of your dark minds; but strive to be prepared in your hearts, be faithful in all things." (*Teachings of the Prophet Joseph Smith,* p. 91.)

A wise man once told me never to read a book I could comprehend in one reading, for a book that could be grasped in one reading was not worth that reading. "Anything that is worth reading once is worth reading numerous times," he said. The temple ordinances, like the scriptures, are worth thousands of readings, and even then we shall not have sounded the depths of their possibilities. Therefore, let us be not discouraged but diligent. The Lord will lead us along.

CHAPTER 4

A Formula for Temple Worship

A powerful and practical formula for temple worship is found in the Savior's words to the Nephites when he visited them after his Resurrection. Jesus spent the day with the Nephites, teaching them numerous beautiful truths, many of which they did not fully understand, particularly the Isaiah verses he concluded with. "I perceive that ye are weak," he told them, "that ye cannot understand all my words which I am commanded of the Father to speak unto you at this time." (3 Nephi 17:2.)

These words express how we often feel as we leave the temple. I know they express how I felt the first time I went to the Los Angeles Temple to receive my own endowment. We are all weak and cannot understand all that the Father has taught us. Occasionally we feel a bit guilty for not comprehending more, but guilt is not the proper response. Occasionally we feel apathetic and attend the temple less often, or we do not pay attention when we do come. These things are even more inappropriate.

What must we do? The Savior tells us to do five things, and the first is very easy: "Therefore, [1] go ye unto your homes, and [2] ponder upon the things which I have said, and [3] ask of the Father, in my name, that ye may understand, and [4] prepare your minds for the morrow, and [5] I come unto you again." (3 Nephi 17:3.) If we do not understand all we see and hear in the temple, we must not be fearful, guilty, or apathetic. We must go home, ponder, pray, prepare, and then return.

Far too often, the first step is the only one we take. We simply go home. Or we do step one and step five. We go home and we return, but we do not ponder, pray, or prepare. We must learn to do all five.

LEARNING TO PONDER

Pondering spiritual things is always an invitation to receive revelation. The scriptures give numerous examples of prophets who have reflected, pondered, meditated, or studied and received glorious spiritual experiences as the result. (See 1 Nephi 11, D&C 76, or D&C 138 as examples.) Pondering requires a deep concentration of thought and focus.

To effectively ponder the temple ordinances, we must be familiar with them. If we want to ponder the scriptures, we can read and reread them, focusing on each word or phrase and how it relates to other truths found elsewhere in the text. We can do this with the temple ordinances only if they are written in our minds and in our hearts, for we cannot study them on a printed page. This occurs the more frequently we participate in them. It is next to impossible to ponder something we are not familiar with.

At times, while listening to the endowment, we may want to pause and reflect about some insight we are discovering. We wish we could stop the session from continuing so we could reflect a little deeper. Sometimes we wish we could write ourselves a note about an insight we are receiving so we could reflect on it more when the ceremony is over. We are afraid we will forget our insight by the time the session is completed. Of course, we can neither write ourselves notes nor stop the session. We must learn to hold the thoughts in our minds and then, in quiet moments in and out of the temple, ponder them and let the Spirit teach us. The more we attend the temple, the more permanently the phrases and words of the endowment rest securely in our minds, where they are available for future pondering.

PRAY FOR UNDERSTANDING

We are told to pray for understanding. How often do we kneel before or after temple attendance and beseech the Lord to teach us some edifying truth from the endowment. The Lord is willing to teach if we will ask. We must allow him, however, to use his own wisdom about when and how to reveal a certain truth. Sometimes he will speak directly to our minds. Sometimes the answer will come in the scriptures. Insight might be presented to us by a spouse, a mother, or a father during a quiet conversation in the celestial room.

"TEACH ONE ANOTHER"

These conversations are completely appropriate and may be the means by which the Lord will answer our prayers for understanding. Occasionally we wonder what we can or cannot say about the ordinances of the temple. Outside the temple, we must use extreme care, speaking only of those things that are in the scriptures or in the official publications of the Church. Even then, we must let this counsel be our guide: "Remember that that which cometh from above is sacred, and must be spoken with care, and by *constraint of the Spirit;* and in this there is no condemnation." (D&C 63:64; emphasis added.)

Inside the temple, among those who are worthy of the ordinances, we may, again with the constraint of the Spirit, teach one another, particularly those in our own families. Some things we do not speak of even within temple walls, but these things are few and obvious. In the context of temple learning, the Lord instructs us in the following words: "As *all have not faith,* seek ye diligently and *teach one another* words of wisdom." (D&C 88:118; emphasis added.) Remember, the temple is called "a *place of instruction* for all those who are called to the work of the ministry in all their several callings and offices; that they may be perfected in the *understanding* of their ministry, in theory, in principle, and in doctrine." (D&C 97:13–14; emphasis added.)

Ideally, the Spirit, using the symbols and the atmosphere of the temple, teaches each person according to his or her needs and in response to the person's individual prayers. But the Spirit can also teach through the words and insights of others. On occasion, Jesus' disciples did not understand the deeper meaning of his parables or figurative language. In private they would ask him the interpretation of these teachings. He rarely refused to explain. His disciples were weak but desirous of learning. We must not be afraid to ask for clarification from the Lord or from each other. When we have insight, it is appropriate, especially within our families, under the guidance of the Spirit, to teach and explain as did the Savior.

"Young people and sometimes older people," said Elder John A. Widtsoe, "will question this or that thing about the temple service. 'Is this or that necessary?' 'Is this or that thing reasonable?' 'Why should I do this or that?' Even though such questions should be needless, *it is best to answer them,* especially if they are asked by those who are untrained and inexperienced and therefore unable to think clearly for themselves." ("Temple Worship," pp. 59–60.) While we are learning to clearly receive instruction through the Holy Ghost, let us, without anxiety, "teach one another words of wisdom" inasmuch as we have wisdom to impart and the Spirit so directs. This sharing may be the Lord's answer to someone's prayers.

Within a family, this sharing of insight can be very uniting. As a teacher in the Church Educational System, I have shared many touching teaching moments with hungry students, but none have been as sweet as when I have sat quietly in the celestial room with my wife, my sisters, my children, or my parents answering questions to the best of my insight and receiving their insights in return. Many of my prayers about the temple have been answered in this manner. In doing this, we must always be careful to respond to the Spirit and never limit the meaning of the temple to our own thoughts. A world of meaning can be discovered if our minds remain open.

Often we must ponder and pray for many years before a certain symbol is revealed. I personally sought guidance about a symbol of the temple for over twenty years. Then one morning, while I was directing a session, the truth rose quietly and beautifully in my mind. When these experiences come to us, they give us confidence and hope. I do not know why the Lord did not answer my prayers about this symbol earlier. Perhaps I was unprepared to receive it, or other experiences in my life made it more powerful when it did come. The Lord is a much better judge in these matters than we are. We must have faith that when the time is right, he will answer our prayers and grant us understanding either directly, through the scriptures, or through the teachings and insights of others, especially those of our family.

All Is Beautiful

As we pray for understanding, we can be assured that everything in the temple is beautiful. "No jot, iota, or tittle of the temple rites is otherwise than uplifting and sanctifying," wrote Elder James E. Talmage. (*The House of the Lord,* p. 84.) I have seen the beauty behind the symbols enough to now know that everything in the temple is beautiful. If I do not yet understand a symbol, I trust that when I do understand it, it will be edifying and wonderful, for that has happened already with other symbols I have pondered and prayed about.

The temptation to reject a symbol as unedifying says much more about our ignorance of its meaning than about the symbol itself. If we understood it, it would be beautiful and powerful. We must constantly pray for understanding and, until it comes, trust that the Lord never presents to the human mind anything that is not edifying.

Preparing the Mind

We are told to prepare our minds to receive the Lord's words. How do we prepare our minds to receive revelation? We have already seen that pondering is an excellent form of preparation. The scriptures teach that humility, also, prepares the mind for revelation. The Lord told the early Saints: "Let him that is ignorant learn wisdom by humbling himself and calling upon the Lord his God, that his eyes may be opened that he may see, and his ears opened that he may hear; for my Spirit is sent forth into the world to enlighten the humble and contrite." (D&C 136:32–33.) Alma saw that the afflictions of the Zoramites had "truly humbled them, and that they were in a preparation to hear the word." (Alma 32:6.)

Hungering after righteousness prepares a mind to receive revelation. The promise is given that if we hunger after righteousness, we will be "filled with the Holy Ghost." (3 Nephi 12:6.) Since the Holy Ghost is the principal teacher in the temple, anything we can do to be "filled" with the Spirit will enhance our learning opportunities. In reality, we will learn relatively little in the temple without the Spirit.

I am a teacher by profession. In my experience, one thing is absolutely irresistible to a teacher—a hungry student. When I see a hungry student, eager to learn, giving me full attention, I want to teach him or her everything I know. I will spend hours with that student, poring over the scriptures and sharing insights. When I have a class where everyone is quiet, alert, and paying strict attention, I teach a much better lesson. I share things I would not ordinarily share. These are wonderful moments that every teacher desires.

When Jesus came to earth, he came as a teacher. I am sure that hungry students are also irresistible to him. Let us go to the temple hungry, with a desire to take in everything and to understand everything. If we go with this attitude, our minds will be prepared to receive whatever the Lord desires us to receive that day. We will leave the temple filled because we went there hungry.

Humility is important, for the proud think they know already. They are not hungry. They come to the temple already filled. The humble know they are empty, that they need nourishment. They come to the temple desiring to feast. The greater the hunger and the more directed it is to be satisfied, the greater the feast will be.

AVOIDING THINGS OFFENSIVE TO THE SPIRIT

Avoiding entertainments, environments, or activities that offend the Spirit helps prepare the mind for revelation. It would be inconsistent, for example, on a Friday night to attend a movie that contained crude or vulgar language or suggestive or violent scenes and then on Saturday morning hope to receive insight in the temple. It would be improper to listen to worldly music whose lyrics or beat was outside the standards set by the Lord while driving to the temple and then be sensitive to the still, small voice once inside its walls.

On occasion our dress and grooming can be offensive. Elder Boyd K. Packer taught this truth from his own experience: "On occasions, when I have performed a marriage in the temple, there has been one there to witness it who obviously has paid little attention to the counsel that the Brethren have given about . . . the extremes of style in clothing, in hair length and arrangement, etc. I have wondered why it is that if such a person was mature enough to be admitted to the temple he would not at once be sensible enough to know that the Lord could not be pleased with those who show obvious preference to follow after the ways of the world." (*The Holy Temple*, p. 74.)

In truth, frequent attendance at the temple protects us from becoming too caught up in the things of the world. President Brigham Young promised the Saints that if they "were in the temple of God working for the living and the dead, [their] eyes and hearts would not be after the fashions of the world nor the wealth of the world." (*Discourses of Brigham Young,* pp. 642–43.)

Arthur Henry King, a former president of the London Temple and a great educator, explained how the scriptures influence our ability to discern between those things that are offensive to the Spirit and those things that are acceptable. The truths he explained relative to the scriptures are equally true about frequent temple worship, for the endowment is one of the purest forms of scripture we have. He said: "When we have the scriptures in our heart and our mind and our soul, then we have a means of measuring all things; we have a means of judging everything else. . . . If we are soaked in the scriptures, we shan't want to look at bad things on our walls or listen to bad music, because they won't fit. We shall intuitively reject them, just as we shall embrace what is good, because we shall have in our minds a firm and sound sense of what is in good taste." (*Abundance of the Heart,* pp. 129–30.)

Consistent temple attendance helps us stay prepared to receive knowledge through the Spirit. It is a powerful motivator and guide to keep the desires, styles, entertainments, and fashions of the world out of our lives. With these distractions of worldliness less dominant, the Spirit provides more and more influence in our thoughts, desires, and appetites, bending them to the will of the Lord and making us receptive to further instruction.

WORK FOR OUR OWN ANCESTORS

Personal genealogical research also seems to prepare our minds for revelation. It helps create an environment that is receptive to spiritual things. I have noticed that when I am doing the work for one of my own or my wife's ancestors, the veil seems thinner, and the inspiration flows more readily. Perhaps that is the result of a deeper commitment to the ordinances because they are being performed for one of our own people. Our concentration seems focused a bit more sharply. At times we may even feel the presence of our ancestors beside us in the temple, teaching us the meaning and relevance of what we are watching and hearing.

President Howard W. Hunter spoke about receiving both halves of a blessing and related the following story to temple work: "Some members . . . engage in temple work but fail to do family history research on their own family lines. Although they perform a divine service in assisting others, they lose a blessing by not seeking their own kindred dead as divinely directed by latter-day prophets.

"I recall an experience of a few years ago that is analogous to this condition. At the close of a fast and testimony meeting, the bishop remarked, 'We have had a spiritual experience today listening to the testimonies borne by each other. This is because we have come fasting according to the law of the Lord. But let us never forget that the law consists of two parts: that we fast by abstaining from food and drink and that we contribute what we have thereby saved to the bishop's storehouse for the benefit of those who are less fortunate.' Then he added, 'I hope no one of us will leave today with only half a blessing.'

"I have learned that those who engage in family history research and then perform the temple ordinance work for those whose names they have found will know the additional joy of receiving both halves of the blessing. . . .

"What a glorious thing it is for us to have the privilege of going to the temple for our own blessings. Then after going to the temple for our own blessings, what a glorious privilege to do the work for those who have gone on before us. This aspect of temple work is an unselfish work. Yet whenever we do temple work for other people, there is a blessing that comes back to us." (*Ensign,* February 1995, pp. 4–5.)

Perhaps part of the other half of the blessing is increased receptivity to the spiritual promptings that open up the beautiful symbols.

WE MUST RETURN

The last aspect of our formula is to return. We must return as often as our circumstances permit. In frequent repetition, the layers of symbolic meaning are revealed. How often we can return varies from person to person. The Lord understands our limitations of time and distance.

I live about ten minutes from the Jordan River Temple. Obviously, the Lord would expect me to return more frequently than the families I knew in the mission field in France. I believe he considers these things and blesses us with insight, truth, and knowledge accordingly. He will touch the memory of those who cannot come as often and increase the understanding they receive, even if they can attend only once a year. He will magnify us according to our efforts and limitations. But for those of us who have the means to go more often, where "much is given much is required." (D&C 82:3.)

This, then, is the formula. When we feel weak and cannot understand all the words of the Father, let us go home, where we will ponder, pray, and prepare our minds. Then let us return frequently to the Lord's house, where our weakness in understanding can be strengthened by the Holy Spirit, who serves as a private tutor in all sacred things.

CHAPTER 5

When Our Souls Are Calm

Sometimes the truths we learn in the temple are not taught through symbols. Often they come through the whisperings of the Spirit because our souls have been calmed through the serenity of the Lord's house. We cry out to the Lord in our anxiety, but most frequently he answers us when our minds and hearts are quiet. The temple creates an environment conducive to the Spirit, and we can be taught directly, perhaps even by those for whom we officiate.

I recall going to the temple for two different people who lived in vastly different situations. One was a man of great nobility; the other was a slave owned by one of my ancestors. I remember feeling pleased that I had a noble line in my family, and yet as I did the work for my ancestor, I sensed his embarrassment at my using his earthly title during the ordinances. It was as if he said to me: "These things have no relevance to us here. We do not think of them anymore. They are forgotten vestiges of the honors of mortal life."

I sensed as he was ordained to the Melchizedek Priesthood that he considered it the supreme honor of his life, worth more than all the titles he had carried during his mortal existence. I carried these thoughts with me throughout the endowment session. I had in my own life recently lost what I thought was a position of respect and honor and was mourning a bit over its loss.

My impressions that day effectively cured me of my sadness. And since then, I have always looked at the honors of men, whether I received them or was denied them, in a much different light. I had found comfort in an earthly trial because the temple had calmed my soul and allowed me to be taught from beyond the veil.

From the slave I learned the joy of total consecration of self to the Lord. This man had spent his whole earthly existence forced to give his time, labor, and life to a worldly master. I sensed his delight and gratitude that he could now freely give his whole soul, his heart, and all his time, energy, and talents to a heavenly master. I almost envied this unqualified release of his will to God. This was not slavery; it was not even duty. It was a son's full and trusting love, given freely to a Father worthy of its deepest intensity.

I have often wondered if such small gifts of insight and inspiration are not our ancestors' gifts to us in exchange for our time and service for them. They are the sweet rewards, granted freely, for hours of research in libraries and patient labor in temples.

PRACTICAL PROBLEMS

The calming influence of the temple also helps us receive answers to the practical challenges and decisions of our lives. President Ezra Taft Benson said, "By virtue of the sacred priesthood in me vested, . . . I promise you that, with increased attendance in the temples of our God, you shall receive increased personal revelation to bless your life as you bless those who have died." (*Conference Report*, April 1987, p. 108.)

Elder John A. Widtsoe, a brilliant mind in academic circles, received practical knowledge from the temple. "I would rather take my practical problems to the House of the Lord than anywhere else," he said. He shared the following experience with the Saints: "For several years, under a Federal grant with my staff of workers we had gathered thousands of data in the field of soil moisture; but I could not extract any general law running through them. I gave up at last. My wife and I went to the temple that day to forget the failure. In the third endowment room, out of the unseen, came the solution, which has long since gone into print." (*In a Sunlit Land*, p. 177.)

If the Lord will reveal solutions about soil moisture, surely he will give us guidance about our marriages, our children, our occupations, or any other decisions or challenges we are facing. "I can think of no better preparation," Elder Widtsoe said on another occasion, "for one's labor on the farm, in the office, wherever it may be, than to spend a few hours in the temple, to partake of its influence and to give oneself unselfishly for the benefit of those who have gone beyond the veil." (*Improvement Era,* October 1952, p. 719.)

We go to the temple when we need help with personal challenges, questions, or problems. In its atmosphere we are more awake to the promptings of the Holy Spirit. In the dedicatory prayer of Solomon's temple, Solomon prayed that the Lord would be gracious, merciful, and hearing when his people came to him with their needs.

"What prayer and supplication," he said, "soever be made by any man, or by all thy people Israel, which shall know every man *the plague of his own heart,* and spread forth his hands to ward this house: Then hear thou in heaven thy dwelling place, and *forgive,* and *do,* and *give* to every man according to his ways, whose heart thou knowest." (1 Kings 8:38–39; emphasis added.)

In Chronicles Solomon's prayer is also recorded. There, different words are used to describe the needs of those who pray at the Lord's house: "Every one shall know *his own sore and his own grief,*" the scripture records. (2 Chronicles 6:29; emphasis added.) In the serene atmosphere of the temple, we may receive the answers to our own sores and our own griefs and find help and healing because our spirits are calm.

CHAPTER 6

"Waters to Swim In"

In the forty-seventh chapter of Ezekiel is a wonderful prophecy that teaches a profound and deeply beautiful lesson on the power and purpose of the temple. It also serves as an excellent illustration of the kind of symbolic teaching found in the House of the Lord. Of all the scriptural teachings on the temple, I love this one the most. Its power lies in its simplicity and in the beauty of its imagery.

Ezekiel saw in vision the temple that will one day be built in Jerusalem on Mt. Zion. When the temple was completed, Ezekiel was brought to the east doors, where he saw a spring of pure water "issued out from under the threshold of the house." (V. 1.) The spring formed a river, which began to flow eastward through the wilderness of Judaea until it finally emptied into the Dead Sea.

The wilderness of Judaea is a dead, sun-baked land where almost nothing grows, but Ezekiel saw that wherever the river flowed, life came to the barren desert. "At the bank of the river," Ezekiel said, "were very many trees on the one side and on the other." (V. 7.) The trees were "for meat, whose leaf shall not fade, neither shall the fruit thereof be consumed: it shall bring forth new fruit . . . because their waters . . . issued out of the sanctuary: and the fruit thereof shall be for meat, and the leaf thereof for medicine." (V. 12.)

The river flowed into the Dead Sea, "which being brought forth into the sea, the waters shall be healed." Ezekiel further saw a "very great multitude of fish. . . . And it shall come to pass, that the fishers shall stand upon it from En-gedi even unto En-eglaim; they shall be a place to spread forth nets; their fish shall be according to their kinds, as the fish of the great sea, exceeding many." (Vv. 8–10.)

Ezekiel describes the river's impact on all it touches with these words: "And it shall come to pass, that *every thing that liveth, which moveth, whithersoever the rivers shall come, shall live* . . . because these waters shall come thither; *for they shall be healed;* and every thing shall live whither the river cometh." (V. 9; emphasis added.)

As we read these words, the Spirit seems to whisper, "What will literally be true, one day, of the Lord's temple in Jerusalem, is true *now,* spiritually, of all the Lord's temples. From the doors of each one a *healing, life-giving* river flows."

Latter-day temples are the source of a powerful, deeply refreshing river. It is a river of peace, revelation, truth, light, and priesthood power. But above all else, it is a river of love. A careful reading of Lehi's dream reveals a second symbol that represents the love of God just as the fruit of the Tree of Life does. Nephi saw that "the rod of iron . . . led [also] to the fountain of living waters, . . . which waters are a representation of the love of God." (1 Nephi 11:25.) This fountain of love flows from the doors of the temples.

We learn from Ezekiel that the water of the river does two things to everything it touches: it gives life and it heals. The life it produces will not "fade," and that which it heals will live forever. The temple's flowing water will heal and give life to our marriages. It will give life to and heal our families. The Church will flourish and become strong and vital as will our individual lives as we plant ourselves near its banks and draw its moisture into our souls.

Doctrine and Covenants 97 speaks of the temple's "pure stream, that yieldeth much precious fruit." If Zion draws continually from that stream, "she shall prosper, and spread herself and become . . . very great . . . and the nations of the earth shall honor her, and shall say: Surely Zion is the city of our God, and surely Zion cannot fall, neither be moved out of her place, for God is there, and the hand of the Lord is there." (Vv. 9, 18–19.)

MEASURE THE DEPTH

In his vision, Ezekiel is instructed to wade into the river and measure its depth. The first time he enters it, "the waters were to the ankles." Now, an ankle-deep river is nothing to get excited about, but Ezekiel is instructed to walk down the bank a little farther and wade in again. This time "the waters were to the knees." He is told to continue down the bank and measure the depth again. "The waters were to the loins."

Ezekiel's last description of the river's depth contains a beautifully symbolic truth of what the temple can become for all of us if we wade into its waters again and again. "It was a river that I could not pass over: for the waters were risen, *waters to swim in,* a river that could not be passed over." (Ezekiel 47:3–5.) The water is now over his head, and he can immerse himself in its cool freshness.

The first time we enter a temple, we barely get our feet wet. We are barely introduced to the Lord's light and love. What a tragedy it is when members of the Church judge the temple to be shallow or not deeply refreshing based on that first experience. Yet all of us know that on a hot summer day, wading even ankle deep in a cool stream brings instant refreshment and a hesitancy to leave the flowing water to return to our shoes. In light of this, it is not difficult to feel Moses' sense of wonder when he was told to "put off thy shoes from off thy feet, for the place whereon thou standest is holy ground." (Exodus 3:5.) Elder Widtsoe cautioned that it is not fair "to pass opinion on temple worship after one day's participation followed by an absence of many years. The work should be repeated several times in quick succession, so that the lessons of the temple may be fastened upon the mind." ("Temple Worship," p. 64.) Little do the casual waders know that down the river, if they will patiently persist, are life-giving, healing "waters to swim in." For the water rises each time we wade. Little do they realize the power of those waters to heal the disharmony of our lives, our families, and eventually the world.

If we understand little or feel little the first time we enter the temple, at all cost let us not abandon the river. We must continue down the bank and wade in again and again. If we do that, we will feel the waters rise until they are over our heads, and we can plunge deeply into the refreshing, life-giving, healing waters of God's love and light. As we continue to wade in again and again, our understanding of the Lord's great plan of mercy and happiness as taught through the temple symbols will rise also. If you feel you are understanding the temple ceremonies at an ankle-deep level, do not despair. Wade in again and again and again. In time you will feel the water rise and your understanding deepen. When talking with children about the temple, I often tell them about Ezekiel's river. Their eyes are full of wonder, delight and anticipation at the thought that one day they too will be able to swim in Heavenly Father's river. We, who are older, can learn a great deal from their eagerness.

"ONE HEART AND ONE MIND"

Immersed in that loving light, we can become one, as Jesus and his Father are one. Jesus taught the Saints of this dispensation, "If ye are not one ye are not mine." (D&C 38:27.) Only the temple can make us one. It can create a Zion people who will be, as the scripture describes, "of one heart and one mind." (Moses 7:18.)

Think of all the unities we are taught in the Lord's house, both literally and through its most sacred symbols. Its healing, life-giving power will "seal" husband to wife for eternity and make them one. It will bind parent to child, brother to brother, and sister to sister and make them one. It will "weld" the living to the dead through countless generations into a "whole and complete and perfect" chain. (See D&C 128:18.) And most important of all, it will allow all humanity to embrace God, to know him as their Father, and to become "of one heart and one mind" with him. With the temple we cannot fail to build Zion; without it we can never become true disciples of the Lord Jesus Christ. All of these unities are implied in the beautiful greeting described in section 88 of the Doctrine and Covenants, which is a critical section in the development of latter-day temple worship: "Art thou a brother or brethren? I salute you in the name of the Lord Jesus Christ, in token or remembrance of the everlasting covenant, in which covenant I receive you to fellowship, in a determination that is fixed, immovable, and unchangeable, to be your friend and brother through the grace of God in the bonds of love, to walk in all the commandments of God blameless, in thanksgiving, forever and ever. Amen." (V. 133.)

I know of no more beautiful greeting in print. It surely has deep significance to the unity we are taught and that is created in the Lord's house. Through the healing, life-giving power of the temple, husbands and wives, parents and children, brothers and sisters, living and dead, all nations and races will be able to so greet each other.

PART 3

HOUSE OF REFUGE

Our Father, may peace abide in all the homes of Thy Saints; may holy angels guard them; may they be encompassed by Thine arms of love . . . and may the tempter and the destroyer be removed far from them. . . . Heavenly Father, when Thy people . . . are oppressed and in trouble, surrounded by difficulties or assailed by temptation and shall turn their faces towards this Thy holy house and ask Thee for deliverance, for help, for Thy power to be extended in their behalf, we beseech Thee to look down from Thy holy habitation in mercy and tender compassion upon them, and listen to their cries.

(SALT LAKE TEMPLE DEDICATORY PRAYER.)

CHAPTER 7

Frequently, Constantly, Consistently

When I moved to Utah ten years ago, my children were entering their teenage years. Having taught teenagers in seminary, I knew how critical the next years would be, for during these years we win or lose so many battles for the souls of men. The more I thought about the world my children were growing up in and the pressures and opposition arrayed against them, the more anxious I felt.

I went to the temple one afternoon to seek guidance about my children. The calm, loving spirit of the temple seemed to magnify my natural love for my family, and I found myself offering a deeply sincere prayer filled with desire for my children. I told the Lord I was willing to offer any sacrifice if he would protect my children from Satan's power and bless them with his Spirit until they could come to his house and receive their own endowment. I do not think I offered a unique prayer. It is the uttered and unuttered prayer of every true Latter-day Saint parent, and I think most parents would give the Lord the sacrifice he required.

As I sat in the temple, an answer was given in which the required sacrifice was revealed to me. I thought the Lord would demand some great thing for the blessing I was asking, and had it been some great thing, I believe I would have been willing to fulfill it. Often we are more willing to do the great things than the small, everyday acts of obedience and sacrifice that comprise living the gospel.

However, the Spirit simply whispered: "This is the sacrifice I ask of you. Be in this house *frequently, constantly,* and *consistently,* and the promised protection you seek, which this house has the power to bestow, will be extended to those you love." For that blessing alone I would be in the temple as often as I could.

At first I thought this counsel was unique to me, but I came to realize as I read and studied the scriptures that it is a promise with much broader application. I found this promise again and again in both the scriptures and in the words of our living prophets and apostles. It was not a special request and promise to me, but one that was extended to all the Saints in behalf of those they love.

"UNSEEN ANGELS"

President Ezra Taft Benson counseled us to "make the temple a sacred home away from our eternal home." He then explained the power the temple can generate in a morally deteriorating world: "This temple will be a standing witness that the power of God can *stay the powers of evil in our midst.* Many parents, in and out of the Church, are concerned about protection against a cascading avalanche of wickedness which threatens to engulf Christian principles. . . . There is a power associated with the ordinances of heaven—even the power of godliness—which can and *will thwart the forces of evil* if we will be worthy of those sacred blessings. This community will be protected, our families will be protected, *our children will be safeguarded* as we live the gospel, visit the temple, and live close to the Lord. (*The Teachings of Ezra Taft Benson,* p. 256; emphasis added.)

Elder Boyd K. Packer taught: "No work is more of a protection to this Church than temple work and the genealogical research which supports it. No work is more spiritually refining. No work we do gives us more power. No work requires a higher standard of righteousness." But the work, although demanding, carries with it wonderful benefits. "Our labors in the temple," Elder Packer continued, "cover us with a *shield and a protection,* both individually and as a people." (*The Holy Temple,* p. 265; emphasis added.)

George Q. Cannon promised the Saints that when "other temples are completed, there will be an increase of power bestowed upon the people of God, and . . . they will, thereby, be better fitted to go forth and *cope with the powers of darkness* and with the evils that exist in the world." (*Journal of Discourses* 14:126; emphasis added.)

"Men grow mighty under the results of temple service," Elder Widtsoe testified; "women grow strong under it; the community increases in power; until the *devil has less influence* than he ever had before." ("Temple Worship," p. 51; emphasis added.)

"If we go into the temple," President Joseph Fielding Smith said, "we raise our hands and covenant that we will serve the Lord and observe his commandments and keep ourselves unspotted from the world. If we realize what we are doing then the endowment will be a *protection* to us all our lives—a protection which a man who does not go to the temple does not have." ("The Pearl of Great Price," *Utah Genealogical and Historical Magazine,* July 1930, p. 103; emphasis added.)

Elder Vaughn J. Featherstone promised "that all who faithfully attend to temple work" will have "*unseen angels watch over [their] loved ones when satanic forces tempt them.*" (In Royden G. Derrick, *Temples in the Last Days,* p. 103; emphasis added.)

Harold B. Lee taught, "We talk about security in this day, and yet we fail to understand that . . . we have standing the holy temple wherein we may find the symbols by which power might be generated that will *save this nation from destruction.*" (*Conference Report,* April 1942, p. 87; emphasis added.)

These statements and others similar to them have been a constant source of comfort and hope to me. They are a reminder to return often to the temple, not only for my own edification or the salvation of the dead but also for the protection and blessing of my children.

CHAPTER 8

In the Time of Trouble

The scriptures frequently teach the protecting power associated with the house of the Lord. "We need simply remember," Elder John A. Widtsoe affirmed, "that the story of ancient Israel, the chosen people of God, centers upon their temples." ("Temple Worship," p. 53.) More examples than we have time to present proves the connection between the temple and the saving power of Jehovah. A few examples, both ancient and modern, however, will be instructive.

In the Old Testament, David assures that "in the time of trouble [the Lord] shall hide [us] in his pavilion: in the secret of his tabernacle shall he hide [us]; he shall set [us] up upon a rock." (Psalm 27:5.) In another psalm David calls the Lord "our *shield*" and then adds, "for a day in thy courts is better than a thousand. I had rather be a door-keeper in the house of my God, than to dwell in the tents of wickedness. For the Lord God is a sun and *shield*: . . . no good thing will he withhold from them that walk uprightly." (Psalm 84:9–11; emphasis added.)

A Prevailing and Combined Enemy

In the Doctrine and Covenants, the Lord explains to the Saints the condition of the world as the final days commence: "All flesh is corrupted before me; and the powers of darkness *prevail* upon the earth . . . and all eternity is pained, and the angels are waiting the great command to reap down the earth . . . and, behold, the enemy is *combined*." (D&C 38:11–12; emphasis added.) How do we as Saints and parents stand against a prevailing and combined (or organized) enemy? How can we keep our children and grandchildren from being overcome by such forces?

The Lord never describes a problem in the scriptures without also giving a solution. Notice how the words in Joseph Smith's dedicatory prayer of the Kirtland Temple match the words from section 38: "We ask thee, Holy Father, to establish the people that shall worship, and honorably hold a name and standing in this thy house, to all generations and for eternity; that no weapon formed against them shall prosper; . . . that no *combination* of wickedness shall have power to rise up and *prevail* over thy people *upon whom thy name shall be put* in this house." (D&C 109:24–26; emphasis added.) Those who have the name of the Father placed upon them need not fear the "prevailing, combined" forces of evil.

THE NAME OF THE FATHER

Echoes of this doctrine are heard resounding from the Old and the New Testaments. In Revelation, John sees four angels holding back the winds of destruction previous to the Second Coming. A fifth angel appears with "the seal of the living God" and instructs the four angels not to unleash the winds until he has "sealed the servants of God in their foreheads." (Revelation 7:1–9.) Later we learn that the seal written in the forehead is the "Father's name." (Revelation 14:1.) "And they shall see his face and his name shall be in their foreheads." (Revelation 22:4.) A quick look in a thesaurus gives us four interesting words interchangeable with *seal.* They are *mark, sign, symbol,* and *token.* In using this imagery, John is alluding to two similar events recorded in the Old Testament: the Passover at the time of Moses, and a vision given to Ezekiel prior to the Babylonian captivity.

In the book of Exodus, the children of Israel are protected from the "destroyer" (Exodus 12:23) by having their doors marked with the blood of a lamb: "When he seeth the blood upon the lintel, and on the two side posts, the Lord will pass over the door, and will not suffer the destroyer to come in unto your houses to smite you." (Exodus 12:23.) In Hebrew the words "pass over" carry the connotation of "warding off a blow or opposing the threatened entrance of an enemy." (See *Wilson's*

Old Testament Word Studies, pp. 303–4.) This episode in Israel's history was to teach them that the atoning blood of Christ protects those who have faith in him from the power of Satan, who is a "destroying angel." The Savior's atonement will oppose Satan's entry and ward off his blows.

A similar pattern is found in the book of Ezekiel. Ezekiel sees in vision six men come to Jerusalem. Five of them come with "a slaughter weapon in his hand; and one man among them [the sixth] was clothed with linen, with a writer's inkhorn by his side." The man clothed with linen is a priesthood bearer. In this story *the priesthood* places the mark, sign, or seal upon the foreheads of the righteous. The Lord calls to the "man clothed with linen, which had the writer's inkhorn by his side; and the Lord said unto him, Go through the midst of the city . . . and set a mark upon the foreheads of the men that sigh and that cry for all the abominations that be done in the midst thereof. And to the others he said in mine hearing, Go ye after him through the city, and smite . . . and begin at my sanctuary." (Ezekiel 9:2–6.) The city is then destroyed, all but those who have the mark upon their foreheads.

It is interesting that in the last days, the final cleansing of the earth also begins at the Lord's house: "Upon my house shall it begin, and from my house shall it go forth, saith the Lord; first among those among you, saith the Lord, who have professed to know my name and have not known me, and have blasphemed against me in the midst of my house, saith the Lord." (D&C 112:25–26.)

In all three examples, Revelation, Exodus, and Ezekiel, a mark or seal of some sort was placed upon those who were to be protected from the forces of destruction. We learn from the book of Revelation that in our day that mark or seal will be the "name of the Father." We learn from the dedicatory prayer of the Kirtland Temple that the name of the Father is placed upon those who "worship, and honorably hold a name and standing in" the Lord's house. In the dedicatory prayer Joseph Smith also prays that the Lord's "servants may go forth from this house armed with thy power, and that *thy name may be upon them, and thy glory may be round about them, and thine angels have charge over them.*" (D&C 109:22; emphasis added.) The threatened entry of the enemy will be opposed for those who have received the Father's name. "Unseen angels" will "have charge over them." Worshiping in the temple will be as important in our day as it was for the children of Israel to mark their doorways with lamb's blood when the destroying angel passed through Egypt.

I do not wish to suggest there is some mystical manner in which we receive the name of the Father in the temple. We must be wise as we interpret and apply symbolic language. The early Israelites were told by Moses to "bind" the commandment to "love the Lord thy God with all thine heart, and with all thy soul, and with all thy might, . . . for a sign upon thine hand, and . . . as frontlets between thine eyes." (Deuteronomy 6:5–8.) In other words, the love and worship of God was to be constantly before their eyes, and their whole lives were to be guided by that love. They would have, in essence, an "eye single to the glory of God." (D&C 4:5.)

When we love and serve God with *all* our heart, soul, and might, we are truly his children. His name is upon us, just as the name of my own earthly father is upon me. We belong to his family and carry his name. Where, if not in the temple, do we as members of the Church promise that we will love and serve God with all our heart, soul, and might? Where are our eyes directed so completely to the glory of the Lord? When we make and strive to keep our covenants, his name is upon us. Then we need not fear the powers of the destroyer. The destroyer will pass us over. He cannot prevail, even though his forces are combined. His threatened entry into our homes and lives will be opposed.

In Revelation, John promised the Saints from Philadelphia that, if they overcame the temptations of their day, the Lord would make them "a pillar in the temple . . . [to] go no more out." Once they were in the temple, the Savior said, he would "write upon [them] the name of my God, and the name of the city of my God, which is new Jerusalem, . . . and I will write upon [them] my new name." (Revelation 3:12.) Here again we see the relationship of temple worship to the name of God. But in order to receive this great blessing, we must overcome temptation enough to enter the temple. Once worthy to enter, we seek to become a "pillar" in the Lord's house, someone he can place weight upon, someone who is steady, strong, and constant.

TRUE WORSHIP

It might be helpful, in light of the greatness of the Lord's promised protection, to return to section 109 of the Doctrine and Covenants and examine a bit more closely what we need to do to have the name of the Father put upon us. Merely attending the temple may not be sufficient. Verse 24 states that we must do two things:

1. We must "worship" the Father in the temple.

2. We must "honorably hold a name and standing" in the temple.

Worshiping God in his house means more than just going to the temple or "doing sessions." True worship is emulation or imitation. I remember once preparing a lesson on the third chapter of Helaman while lying on my bed. I had my red and blue pencils out and was underlining and making notes to myself. My six-year-old son watched me for a moment, then ran to his bedroom and returned with his own copy of the Book of Mormon. He positioned himself next to me, assuming my exact posture, and began to "color" in his Book of Mormon also. I was vaguely aware of what he was doing because I had seen him color in his scriptures before. About half an hour later, I finished my lesson and glanced at his book. There before my eyes was an exact duplicate of my markings in Helaman chapter 3. He had found the same page, underlined the same verses, drawn the same arrows, highlighted the same words, and even started to write some of the notes I had written in my margins, but of course his writing was much too big, so he only managed to get the first three words on the page.

There was a spot on my page where the red pencil had bled onto the next. It was very faint, so my son had colored the spot in his book and then erased it so it would look similar. When he saw me examining his page, he put his head down and almost started to cry. "What's the matter, son?" I asked him. In a timid voice he answered, "My lines are not as straight as yours are."

My son taught me the greatest lesson on the meaning of worship I have ever received. When we worship the Savior in his temple, we study carefully all that we learn about him there. Then we try to follow exactly every quality that is shown us. We want to walk, talk, forgive, love, obey, bless, pray, and endure as he did. Our "lines" will not be as straight as his are, but our truest efforts will always be acceptable to him. When we emulate the Savior, as we come to perceive him in the temple ordinances, we discover the meaning of true worship, and, of course, there is no better way to emulate him than to do the selfless, vicarious work for the dead that they cannot do for themselves, just as he vicariously gave his life for ours.

GROWING UP IN THE LORD'S HOUSE

In the fifteenth verse of Doctrine and Covenants 109, Joseph Smith prays that the Saints "may grow up in thee" while in the temple. When we are baptized into the Church, we are said to be "born again." We become innocent as a baby through the Savior's sacrifice. He is, therefore, the "father" of our rebirth. We then need to be nourished on the milk of his doctrines until maturity allows us to feast on the meat.

God does not intend for his newborn babes in Christ to remain babies; he wants us to grow up and reach full maturity. He desires to teach, protect, and guard us while we mature, just as any parent does. Each one must come to "the knowledge of the Son of God, unto a *perfect man, unto the measure of the stature of the fulness of Christ.*" (Ephesians 4:13; emphasis added.) Since Jesus is the father of our rebirth, and the temple is his house, he invites all of his children to "grow up" under his roof, where they can receive his guiding care. Here we can watch him and learn to emulate him.

If you think about it, next to our own homes, we have freer access to the temple than almost any other building. Even the chapels are closed to us more often than the temple. Of course, we must carry a key to the front door of the temple just as we carry a key to the front door of our own homes. The key to the temple is a recommend, but once worthy of a recommend, we can enter the temple any time we like, from five in the morning to ten at night, and we can stay as long as we wish while the temple is open. The temple is our second home. We are invited to "grow up there."

There, in his house, we learn how to reach the "full measure" of his stature, just as children in an earthly home learn by watching their parents' examples. In the temple we observe the Savior's perfect example and learn to walk in his footsteps. Without the temple we remain spiritual children. With the temple we can learn to emulate the mature image of the Savior.

"When I was a child," Paul wrote, "I spake as a child, I understood as a child, I thought as a child: but when I became a man, I put away childish things." (1 Corinthians 13:11.) In the temple we learn to "put away" our childish things and reach spiritual maturity. This is how we worship the Lord in his house.

HONORABLY HOLD A NAME AND STANDING

The Kirtland Temple dedicatory prayer also instructs us that we must "honorably hold a name and standing" in the temple. In order to "grow up" and worship, we need a key to the front door. Each year we are given the opportunity to receive a temple recommend. It allows us to hold a name and standing in the Lord's house. But we must not only obtain a recommend; we must also "honorably" hold it.

The word *honor* has many connotations. It means to obey, to trust, to give glory to, to respect, and to conduct one's affairs with integrity. All of these meanings help us understand how to honorably maintain our standing in the temple.

It is now possible for our young people to receive group recommends that last for a year. How wonderful it would be if every member of the Church could honorably hold a recommend each year from age twelve to the day he or she died. What great lesson could we teach our children if we encouraged them to hold a group recommend throughout their youth and to perform baptisms for the dead as often as circumstances would allow?

The word *standing* implies frequent attendance. The dictionary's definitions of standing are "length of time or duration; permanent and unchanging; not movable; stationary; high reputation or esteem." (*The American Heritage Dictionary.*) All these meanings bear on the Lord's words in the Doctrine and Covenants and imply the constant, continual use of the recommend.

In conclusion, if we desire the promised protection of the Father's name, we must receive our temple recommends, hold them honorably, and use them frequently, not merely to attend the temple but also to worship there.

CHAPTER 9

Isaiah's Prophetic Promise

A wonderfully comforting scripture in chapter 4 of Isaiah bears on the protecting power of the Lord's house. Speaking of the latter days, the Lord promises to "create upon *every dwelling place* of mount Zion, and upon her *assemblies,* a cloud and smoke by day, and the shining of a flaming fire by night: for upon all the glory shall be a defence.

"And there shall be a *tabernacle* for a shadow in the daytime from the heat, and for a place of refuge, and for a covert from storm and from rain." (Vv. 5–6; emphasis added.)

"Every dwelling place" is every home, and the "assemblies" are every ward and stake. Isaiah alludes to the pillar of fire that guided and protected Israel as they wandered in the wilderness. At that time, however, the pillar was over only the tabernacle, not over each family's tent. But in the last days each "dwelling place" will have the promised protection if we are worthy of it through faithfulness to our covenants. If we have the eyes to see, we can stand in front of our homes and know that, spiritually speaking, the Lord's glory, his pillar, is above them and will defend them. This is also true of our wards and stakes.

We are told in the scriptures that it is the will of the Lord "that all . . . who call on [his] name, and worship [him] . . . should gather together and stand in holy places" when the great problems of the last days begin to unfold. (D&C 101:22.) That does not mean to find a holy place and stay there. Rather, it means to "make a stand" or defend a position.

In battle, often a general will tell his soldiers to defend a certain position at all costs. "Here we will make our stand!" he might say to them. That is what the Lord is saying to us: "Latter-day Saints, make your stand against evil in holy places. Defend these positions at all costs!"

There are three holy places Isaiah describes. They are the home, the stake, and the temple. In these places we can defeat Satan. These positions we must defend. In them we will make our stand. We can triumph over the adversary only if we protect the home, the stake, and the temple. They, in turn, will give us protection. Here we will have the Lord's glory to defend and help us. We simply cannot allow the forces of the world to invade these three sacred places. If we do, the battle, indeed the war, will be lost.

A SHADOW FROM THE HEAT

Isaiah speaks of a tabernacle or temple. He gives three images to describe what the temple will do for the Latter-day Saints. The temple is a "shadow in the daytime from the heat." Sometimes the world is like a hot summer's day beating down on us. There are no clouds in the sky and no relief in sight. We search anxiously for a place of shade to shield us from the burning heat of the sun. When the world's heat becomes oppressive, the Lord says to us: "Come into the shade of my house. Be refreshed! Be renewed! No burning heat will reach you here. Drink from my fountain. Swim in my river, and you will be able to return to the challenges of life, prepared to meet them."

A PLACE OF REFUGE

Isaiah calls the temple a "place of refuge." This is an image of battle and war. In life we fight daily against the forces of Satan and temptation. When we feel we are about to be swept away by the adversary's powerful advance, the Lord says: "Come into my place of refuge. Rest awhile. No enemy shaft can find you here. Feast from my table. Be strengthened and invigorated. Let your fears subside. The battle does not rage within these walls. Then you can return to the battle and wield your sword with confidence and the assurance of ultimate victory." It is no coincidence that the walls of the Salt Lake Temple are crowned with battlements. They suggest a fortress where the forces of evil cannot penetrate and where the righteous can seek the safety of unconquerable walls.

COVERT FROM STORM

Isaiah calls the temple a "covert from the storm and from rain." Life's storms also beat upon us, threatening to "drag [us] down to the gulf of misery and endless wo." We look around for shelter when Satan sends forth "his mighty winds, yea, his shafts in the whirlwind, yea, when all his hail and his mighty storm . . . [beat] upon [us]" and buffet our faith. (Helaman 5:12.) The Lord calls to us through the wind and the lightning: "Come into my house and out of the storm. Wipe the rain off you, sit in the warmth of my eternal fire. No unhallowed gust can reach you here. When you are cheered and comforted by my house, the storm will not seem so black nor the sunshine so far away."

"Shadow." "Refuge." "Covert." Each word offers powerful images of hope and inspiration to those who live when darkness "prevails" and the enemy is "combined." We must not try to bear the heat, or fight the battle, or bend against the storm without accepting a gracious Father's invitation to be renewed occasionally by the cool, safe, and sheltered protection of temple walls.

CUMBERED, TROUBLED, AND CAREFUL

Once when Jesus came to Bethany, Mary and Martha prepared a meal for him. Mary sat at Jesus' feet to be taught by him, leaving Martha to "serve alone." The scriptures say that Martha was "*cumbered* about much serving." She turned to the Lord and asked him to tell Mary to help her. Gently, Jesus turned to Martha and said, "Martha, Martha, thou art *careful and troubled* about many things: but one thing is *needful:* and Mary hath chosen that good part, which shall not be taken away from her." (Luke 10:38–42; emphasis added.) There are times for service and there are times to sit quietly and listen. We need not choose between Martha's devotion and Mary's eagerness.

I know in my own life I often feel cumbered, troubled, and careful about many things. They need not be storms or battles or burning days. They are not negative things or temptations. Sometimes our service weighs us down. Martha was not doing anything wrong; she was serving her Lord. But in spite of her service, something else was also "needful."

More times than we like to admit, we "need" to sit quietly and rest while we listen to the words of our Lord and Master. As strange as it sounds, we sometimes need to stop serving in order to listen more. Eventually, this will help us serve more effectively. In the Kirtland Temple dedicatory prayer, we are told that in the temple we would be prepared to "obtain every *needful thing*." (D&C 109:15; emphasis added.) Obviously "every needful thing" encompasses our *need* to sit, rest, and listen at the feet of Jesus. This is "that good part which shall not be taken away."

Often we spend many hours fulfilling our various church callings, family responsibilities, and occupational duties, all of which are important. But we feel cumbered, troubled, and careful. Months pass, and we have not sat quietly at the feet of the Lord to be refreshed. In the temple we are invited to lay the burdens down, to sit, to rest, and to listen, because it is "needful." From an eternal perspective, it is more needful than PTA conferences, Relief Society service projects, Scout camps, soccer games, car pools, or priesthood leadership meetings. It is needful so we will not fail to make our "stand" against the destroyer.

CHAPTER 10

"No Might against This Great Company"

If we are tempted to minimize the temple's protecting power, we need only look through the scriptures to find additional testimony of its influence in earlier trying times. When Jehoshaphat, king of Judah, faced a strong combination of surrounding armies against which he knew his people could not stand, he called a "fast throughout all Judah," then went up to the temple to pray. Notice the words of his prayer: "O Lord God of our fathers, art not thou God in heaven? . . . Art not thou our God, who didst drive out the inhabitants of this land before thy people Israel, and gavest it to the seed of Abraham thy friend forever? And they dwelt therein, and have built thee a sanctuary therein for thy name, saying, If, when evil cometh upon us, as the sword, judgment, or pestilence, or famine, we stand before this house, and in thy presence, (for thy name is in this house,) and cry unto thee in our affliction, then thou wilt hear and help. . . . O our God, . . . we have no might against this great company that cometh against us; neither know we what to do: but our eyes are upon thee." (2 Chronicles 20:3–12.)

The Lord hearkened to the prayer of Jehoshaphat, telling him to "stand . . . still, and see the salvation of the Lord" (2 Chronicles 20:17), which they did the next day. The "great company" began to fight against themselves, and in their own bitter quarrels they left Judah alone. What the Lord was willing to do for Jehoshaphat's people, he will surely do for us when we face "prevailing, combined" enemies and forces we feel "we have no might against."

61

FIRST MONTH, FIRST YEAR

At another desperate time of Judah's history, Hezekiah came to the throne. Darkness was prevailing then as now in the form of the might of Assyria. This and other forces threatened to destroy his people. Part of the northern tribes had already gone into Assyrian captivity. Judah itself was in a state of apostasy. In these challenging circumstances, Hezekiah's first official act as a young king of twenty-five is significant.

"He in the *first year* of his reign, in the *first month,* opened the doors of the house of the Lord. . . . And he brought in the priests and the Levites . . . and said unto them . . . Sanctify now yourselves, and sanctify the house of the Lord. . . . For our fathers have . . . turned away their faces from the habitation of the Lord, and turned their backs. Also they have shut up the doors of the porch, and put out the lamps, and have not burned incense nor offered burnt offerings in the holy place unto the God of Israel. . . . My sons, be not now negligent: for the Lord hath chosen you to stand before him, to serve him, and that ye should minister unto him, and burn incense." (2 Chronicles 29:2–11; emphasis added.)

Members of the Church today face great challenges, both temporal and spiritual. Have we, on occasion, also "turned away [our] faces from the habitation of the Lord . . . [and] shut up the doors . . . and put out the lamps." Are we also "negligent"? Often so many pressures demand our time and attention. However, considering the times and the forces arrayed against our families, should we not follow Hezekiah's example and "sanctify the house of the Lord . . . in the *first* year of the *first* month?" (Emphasis added.)

ENTER INTO HIS SANCTUARY

The results of Hezekiah's actions are also instructive. After renewing the temple worship, Hezekiah's people returned to the Lord's house to renew their covenants. Hezekiah "wrote letters also to Ephraim and Manasseh [the northern tribes], that they should come to the house of the Lord at Jerusalem."

At this time, the southern tribe of Judah was separated from, and often at war with, the northern ten tribes led by Ephraim. In spite of this, Hezekiah issued his invitation. "So the posts went with the letters from the king and his princes throughout all Israel and Judah, and according to the commandment of the king, saying, Ye children of Israel, turn again unto the Lord God of Abraham, Isaac, and Israel, and he will return to the remnant of you, that are escaped out of the hand of the kings of Assyria. . . . Now be ye not stiffnecked, as your fathers were, but yield yourselves unto the Lord, and *enter into his sanctuary,* which he hath sanctified for ever." (2 Chronicles 30:1–9; emphasis added.)

Hezekiah's gracious offer went largely unheeded among the northern tribes. As the "posts passed from city to city through the country of Ephraim and Manasseh even unto Zebulun . . . they laughed them to scorn and mocked them." (2 Chronicles 30:10.) How could the simple act of returning to the service and rites of the temple offer protection against the might of Assyria? In the end, only Hezekiah's kingdom and a few individuals from the northern tribes heeded the call.

There is a sad conclusion to the northern tribes' refusal to return to the sanctuary. "In the fourth year [three years later] of king Hezekiah . . . Shalmaneser king of Assyria came up against Samaria [the capital of the northern tribes], and besieged it. And at the end of three years they took it. . . . And the king of Assyria did carry away Israel unto Assyria . . . because they obeyed not the voice of the Lord their God, but transgressed his covenant." (2 Kings 18:9–12.)

This is the beginning of the lost ten tribes. Had they heeded Hezekiah's invitation to return to the Lord's house and there worship Him, the whole history of Israel might have been different.

"ON WHOM DOST THOU TRUST?"

After reducing the northern kingdom of Israel, the Assyrian army also laid siege to Hezekiah in Jerusalem. Full of confidence, the Assyrian emissaries shouted to the defenders on the walls: "What confidence is this wherein thou trustest? Thou sayest, (but they are but vain words,) I have counsel and strength for the war. Now on whom dost thou trust? . . . Ye say unto me, We trust in the Lord our God. . . . Let not Hezekiah deceive you: for he shall not be able to deliver you out of his hand: Neither let Hezekiah make you trust in the Lord, saying, The Lord will surely deliver us. . . . Hath any of the gods of the

nations delivered at all his land out of the hand of the king of Assyria?"
(2 Kings 18:19–33.)

But the people, renewed by their worship and the example of
Hezekiah, "held their peace" and waited for the Lord's deliverance.
(2 Kings 18:36.) When Hezekiah heard the words of the Assyrian messenger and knew there was no logical way he could hold out against
the might of the Assyrian army, he "went into the House of the Lord"
and there offered a deeply touching prayer in behalf of his people. The
Lord responded by assuring Hezekiah that the Assyrians would not
"shoot an arrow" against the city. That night "the angel of the Lord
went out, and smote in the camp of the Assyrians an hundred
fourscore and five thousand. . . . So Sennacherib king of Assyria
departed." (2 Kings 19:1, 32, 35–36.)

We do not now face invading armies, but the forces arrayed against
our families are surely no less dangerous. I firmly believe the Lord will
be willing to offer the same blessings he offered Hezekiah's people if
we also will heed the invitation to "enter into his sanctuary."

A MODERN HEZEKIAH

In light of this powerful Old Testament example, it is interesting
to note a similar pattern in the Doctrine and Covenants. In 1841, the
Lord instructed Joseph Smith to make a proclamation that would be
sent "to all the kings of the world, to the four corners thereof, to the
honorable president-elect, and the high-minded governors of the
nation in which you live, and to all the nations of the earth scattered
abroad. Let it be written in the spirit of meekness and by the power of
the Holy Ghost." (D&C 124:3–4.)

What was to be the central theme of this proclamation? Just as in
Hezekiah's day, it was an invitation to come to the temple and there
find safety from the last days of trial and turmoil. Notice what the Lord
says after instructing Joseph Smith to send the proclamation to all
nations: "The day of my visitation cometh speedily, in an hour when
ye think not of; and *where shall be the safety of my people, and refuge
for those who shall be left of them?* [Remember that Hezekiah's invitation was to the "remnant of you, that are escaped." (2 Chronicles
30:6.)] Awake, O kings of the earth! Come ye, O, come ye, with your

gold and your silver, to the help of my people, *to the house* of the daughters of Zion." This invitation to the kings of the nations was followed by an invitation to all the Saints to come "and build a house to my name, for the Most High to dwell therein." (D&C 124:10–11, 27; emphasis added.)

The invitation was sent. It went largely unheeded by the nations of the world, but the Saints responded and built the Nauvoo Temple and have continued to build temples from that day on. The sobering lesson of Hezekiah's day is being repeated. For the Saints who come to the sanctuary, the Lord's miraculous deliverance from sometimes overwhelming odds and forces can also be expected. Might we, also, not have reason to hope that the enemy will not "shoot an arrow" to strike at the foundations of our families?

THE JACKSON COUNTY LESSON

In the dark days of the Jackson County mobbings, the Saints turned to the Lord for protection and counsel. He gave them one commandment that he promised would cause Zion to "prosper, and spread herself and become very glorious, very great, and very terrible." (D&C 97:18.) What was the commandment? "It is my will that *a house should be built* unto me in the land of Zion, like unto the pattern which I have given you. Yea, let it be built *speedily*, by the tithing of my people. Behold, this is the tithing and the sacrifice which I, the Lord, require at their hands, that there may be a house built unto me for *the salvation of Zion*." (D&C 97:10–12; emphasis added.)

The Saints did not build the temple in Jackson County. The command to build one "speedily" must have sounded to them like a strange demand in light of their situation. Their leaders had been tarred and feathered. Their press had been destroyed and their homes ransacked and burned. Yet the Lord was counseling them to walk into the center of Independence and start laying the foundation of a temple.

I have often wondered what would have happened if all the Saints in Missouri had dropped whatever they were doing, picked up their tools, and marched, en masse, to Independence and started digging foundations. It would have taken tremendous courage, but the history of the Church might have been much different. Let us never underestimate the protective power of the temple. "Every time a temple is dedicated to the Lord," Spencer W. Kimball said, "the darkness pushes farther back, . . . and light comes into the world." (*The Teachings of Spencer W. Kimball*, p. 534.) That light is as necessary (and perhaps more necessary) in our day as it was in times past.

CONSIDER YOUR WAYS

After the Babylonian captivity, the remnant of Israel returned to their land and once again faced tremendous opposition and danger. This, too, was a critical time. Israel's small force faced the power of the worldly elements that surrounded them. They were struggling and poor, and though they had returned specifically to rebuild the temple, it remained in ruins. The Lord told the people to "consider [their] ways. . . . He that earneth wages earneth wages to put it into a bag with holes. . . . Ye looked for much, and, lo, it came to little; and when ye brought it home, I did blow upon it. Why? . . . Because of mine house that is waste, and ye run every man unto his own house." The people felt it was not "time" to build the Lord's house, but they seemed to have "time . . . to dwell in [their] cieled [paneled] houses." (Haggai 1:2–9.)

Haggai's message stirred the spirit of the people, "and they came and did work in the house of the Lord of hosts, their God." (Haggai 1:14.) This reordering of priorities immediately brought the Lord's blessings upon them, both spiritually and temporally. It also brought this comforting promise: "Be strong, all ye people . . . and work; for I am with you . . . my spirit remaineth among you: fear ye not. . . . I will shake all nations, and the desire of all nations shall come: and I will fill this house with glory . . . and *in this place will I give peace.*" (Haggai 2:4–9; emphasis added.) Their commitment to place the Lord's house first solved their other problems, even their financial ones. Perhaps John A. Widtsoe had this story in mind when he promised the Saints: "Whoever seeks to help those on the other side receives help in return in all the affairs of life. I can think of no better preparation for one's labor on the farm, in the office, wherever it may be, than to spend a few hours in the temple, to partake of its influence and to give oneself unselfishly for the benefit of those who have gone beyond the veil." (*Improvement Era,* October 1952, p. 719.)

SO MUCH FOR SO LITTLE

I have often asked my students to write a paper on the 109th section of the Doctrine and Covenants, which is the dedicatory prayer for the Kirtland Temple. Their assignment is to identify every blessing in the prayer that comes to the Saints from temple worship. (I suggest this as a wonderful assignment for anyone who wants to gain a deeper appreciation of the temple.) After completing this list, they are to identify every word or phrase that suggests what they must do to receive those blessings. Their papers are wonderful to read, and I have received many insights from them, but one paper in particular struck me. After listing the blessings she had found and how to receive them, one young lady concluded her paper with these words: "I think it is significant and revealing of the Lord's character that we must do so little to be able to receive so much."

I echo and bear testimony to her words. Our efforts in the temple for ourselves, our families, and our ancestors are infinitely small in comparison to the storehouse of blessings the Lord has promised us if we will participate in the "most glorious of all subjects belonging to the everlasting gospel." (D&C 128:17.) For the Lord's protection alone, all our efforts are repaid.

May this realization prompt all of us to sing as did David: "How amiable are thy tabernacles, O Lord of hosts! My soul longeth, yea, even fainteth for the courts of the Lord. . . . For a day in thy courts is better than a thousand." (Psalm 84:1–2, 10.) "Blessed is the man whom thou choosest, and causest to approach unto thee, that he may dwell in thy courts: we shall be satisfied with the goodness of thy house, even of thy holy temple." (Psalm 65:4.)

PART 4

HOUSE OF ORDER

*Our Father in Heaven . . . we pray that our covenants and contracts which
we make with Thee and with each other may be directed by Thy Holy Spirit,
be sacredly kept by us, and accepted by Thee, and that all the blessings
pronounced may be realized by all Thy Saints who come to these altars,
in the morning of the resurrection of the just.*

(SALT LAKE TEMPLE DEDICATORY PRAYER.)

CHAPTER 11

Much Is Required—
Honoring Our Covenants

The Lord tells us that his house is a house of order. It is the covenants of the temple that create the order in his house and also in his eternal kingdom. "Behold, mine house is a house of order, saith the Lord God, and not a house of confusion. Will I accept of an offering, saith the Lord, that is not made in my name? Or will I receive at your hands that which I have not appointed? And will I appoint unto you, saith the Lord, except it be by law, even as I and my Father ordained unto you, before the world was?" (D&C 132:8–11.)

As we have seen, true temple worship brings a multiplicity of blessings, but they are given conditionally. The Lord states: "Of him unto whom much is given much is required." (D&C 82:3.) Notice that the word is *required*. Sometimes I find myself misquoting this verse by using the word *expected* instead of *required*. But these two words have greatly different meanings. The Lord does not *expect* our devotion; he *requires* it.

We do not speak in detail of the covenants of the Lord's house, for these also are sacred. However, Elder James E. Talmage gave a general description of temple covenants in his book *The House of the Lord:* "The ordinances of the endowment embody certain obligations on the part of the individual, such as covenant and promise to observe the law of strict virtue and chastity, to be charitable, benevolent, tolerant and pure; to devote both talent and material means to the spread of truth and the uplifting of the [human] race; to maintain devotion to the cause of truth; and to seek in every way to contribute to the great preparation that the earth may be made ready to receive her King,— the Lord Jesus Christ. With the taking of each covenant and the assuming of each obligation a promised blessing is pronounced, contingent upon the faithful observance of the conditions." (P. 84.)

Organized, Prepared, Established

All who would receive the wonderful rewards of temple service must make these sacred covenants with the Lord. Indeed, our reception of the promised blessings are contingent upon our faithful keeping of temple covenants. In the dedicatory prayer of the Kirtland Temple, Joseph Smith prayed, "Assist us, thy people, with thy grace, in calling our solemn assembly, that it may be done to thine honor and to thy divine acceptance; and in a manner that we may be found worthy, in thy sight, to secure a fulfilment of the promises which thou hast made unto us, thy people." (D&C 109:10–11.) We secure these promises by strictly maintaining our covenants.

The covenant relationship formed in the temple is beautifully described by the repeated use of three words in section 109. These three words plainly show that each party to the covenant has a responsibility. In verse 8 the Lord instructs his Saints, "*Organize* yourselves; *prepare* every needful thing, and *establish* a house of prayer." (Emphasis added.) We are asked to organize, prepare, and establish ourselves so that temple work can proceed. This is our part of the covenant and includes everything from providing funds for the building of temples to our own individual preparation as determined in a temple recommend interview.

In verses 15 and 24, all three of these words are repeated, only this time as descriptions of what the Lord will do for those who enter his temple and keep their covenants: "Grant, Holy Father, that all those who shall worship in this house may . . . be *organized* according to thy laws, and be *prepared* to obtain every needful thing; . . . We ask thee, Holy Father, to *establish* the people that shall worship, and honorably hold a name and standing in this thy house, to all generations and for eternity." (D&C 109:14–15, 24.) One can readily sense the covenant relationship in these repeated words. If *we* organize, prepare, and establish his house, the *Lord* will also, organize, prepare, and establish us "to all generations and for eternity."

DEAD WORKS OR LIVING ORDINANCES?

In the scriptures the Lord speaks of "dead works." He warns us not to trust in them or we will be disappointed. (See Moroni 8:23; D&C 22:2–3.) A dead work is an ordinance devoid of the Spirit. All ordinances, in order to secure the promises, must be performed by proper authority and sealed by the Holy Ghost. This sealing comes when compliance with the covenants has been accomplished.

If we are not careful, we may so much emphasize being endowed or married in the temple that we give the impression that the blessings are assured automatically. When the Lord gave the revelation on temple marriage, he told the Saints they must "*abide* in [the] covenant" or "*abide* the law" if they expected their marriages to be truly eternal. (D&C 132:19.) According to the dictionary, *abide* means to "wait patiently for, to withstand, to persevere, to continue, to endure, to dwell or sojourn, to conform, to comply with, to remain in one place or state." (*American Heritage Dictionary.*)

All these definitions give meaning to our covenants. We would be foolish to assume that a couple who were married in the temple and then never returned or became unworthy to hold temple recommends would still receive all the promised blessings of the temple ceremony. The possibility for eternal companionship is there, but their work is a "dead" work unless they "abide" in the covenant. If we are not worthy to enter the temple here on earth, surely we deceive ourselves if we think we will be worthy to enter the Lord's eternal kingdom, there to receive all the blessings of the faithful.

NOBODY SEALS AN EMPTY JAR

My wife often cans peaches and pears in the fall. A great deal of work is necessary just to prepare the fruit. Then, once it is prepared, she puts it into jars, places the seals on, twists the lids tightly into place, and sets the jars in boiling water. Then she waits for the seals to set.

She has performed this operation dozens of times with hundreds of jars. In all that time I have never seen her seal an empty jar. Unless the jar is loaded with fruit, a seal is not placed. I doubt if anyone, among the thousands who can fruit every year, has ever sealed an empty jar. There must be something to preserve or the seal has no significance.

The sealing of temple covenants is similar. When we are married at the altars of the temple, the Lord, from one point of view, gives us an empty jar. Then he instructs us to fill it with the wonderful fruits of righteous marriage. As we keep our covenants, returning often to renew them as we work for the dead, the jar begins to fill. As we grow older and our love deepens, we desire to preserve forever all the good we have stored. Our abiding in the covenant allows the Lord to place the seal on our covenant relationship and preserve the fruits of our righteousness for all eternity. This is the same for all temple covenants. Nobody seals an empty jar; neither does the Lord seal empty covenants. First there must be fruit to preserve.

Our attitude toward temple covenants must be serious. We must not enter the temple lightly. One of the greatest sources of sadness I experienced while serving as a bishop was discovering the many couples who had received their endowments, married in the temple, and then become unworthy to return, and who remained so year after year. Often the major obstacle was tithing, and yet how small a percentage of our income is a tenth when compared to all we can receive if we are more faithful? Brigham Young said, "I feel sometimes like lecturing men and women severely, who enter into covenants without realizing the nature of the covenants they make, and who use little or no effort to fulfil them." (*Journal of Discourses* 3:332.)

George Q. Cannon reiterated Brigham Young's feelings with his own testimony: "When the Prophet Joseph first communicated that the Lord had revealed to him the keys of the endowment, I can remember the great desire there was on every hand to understand something about them. . . . How is it now? There is a complete indifference, it may be said, in relation to it. Young people go there stupid, with no particular desire only to get married, without realizing the character of the obligations that they take upon themselves or the covenants that they make and the promises involved in the taking of these covenants. The result is, hundreds among us go to the house of the Lord and receive these blessings and come away without having any particular impression made upon them." (*Gospel Truth* 1:228.)

We must do better than that. Where much is given, much is required. As we keep the covenants we have made in the temple, we will receive the wonderful blessings reserved for those who are faithful.

CHAPTER 12

"Be Consequences What They May"

On April 1, 1838, Abraham Lincoln wrote the following letter from Springfield, Illinois, to a friend of his living in Quincy. Since Lincoln felt he had made a fool of himself, he chose April 1 as the most appropriate day to relate his experience: "In the autumn of 1836 . . . a married lady of my acquaintance, and who was a great friend of mine, being about to pay a visit to her father . . . proposed to me, that on her return she would bring a sister of hers with her, upon condition that I would engage to become her brother-in-law with all convenient dispatch. I, of course, accepted the proposal; for you know I could not have done otherwise, had I really been averse to it; but privately between you and me, I was most confoundedly well pleased with the project. I had seen the said sister some three years before, thought her intelligent and agreeable, and saw no good objection to plodding through life hand in hand with her. Time passed on, the lady took her journey, and in due time returned, sister in company sure enough. This stomached me a little; for it appeared to me, that her coming so readily showed that she was a trifle too willing; but on reflection it occurred to me, that she might have been prevailed on by her married sister to come, without anything concerning me ever having been mentioned to her. . . . All this occurred upon my hearing of her arrival in the neighborhood; for, be it remembered, I had not yet seen her, except about three years previous, as before mentioned.

"In a few days we had an interview, and although I had seen her before, she did not look as my imagination had pictured her. I knew she was over-size, but she now appeared a fair match for Falstaff; I knew she was called an 'old maid', and I felt no doubt of the truth of at least half of the appellation; but now, when I beheld her, I could not for my life avoid thinking of my mother; and this, not from withered features, for her skin was too full of fat, to permit its contracting into wrinkles; but from her want of teeth, weather-beaten appearance in general, and from a kind of notion that ran in my head, that nothing could have commenced at the size of infancy, and reached her present bulk in less than thirty five or forty years; and, in short, I was not all pleased with her. *But what could I do? I had told her sister that I would take her for better or for worse; and I made a point of honor and conscience in all things, to stick to my word, especially if others had been induced to act on it,* which in this case, I doubted not they had, for I was now fairly convinced, that no other man on earth would have her. . . . *Well, thought I, I have said it, and, be consequences what they may, it shall not be my fault if I fail to do it.* At once I determined to consider her my wife; and this done, all my powers of discovery were put to the rack, in search of perfections in her, which might be fairly set-off against her defects." (Carl Sandburg, *Abraham Lincoln: The Prairie Years and the War Years,* p. 59.)

I have wondered every time I read this letter if I would have had Lincoln's integrity had I been in his shoes. I doubt many men would. Most would seek a quick denial through rationalization and excuses. Lincoln, however, was true to his word and asked the woman to marry him. In fact, he asked her several times, but each time he was rejected. He finally gave up and later married Mary Todd, but he remained true to his word throughout his life.

The covenants we make in the temple are surely as important if not more important than the promises we make with one another. How wonderful it would be if each of us could say as did Lincoln, "Well, thought I, I have said it, and be consequences what they may, it shall not be my fault if I fail to do it."

HOLDING YOUR SOUL IN YOUR OWN HANDS

Another example of someone who was unconcerned with consequences is Sir Thomas More. His example is portrayed in one of the
greatest movies ever made, Robert Bolt's *A Man for All Seasons*. It tells
the story of Sir Thomas More's eventual death for refusing to take an
oath supporting Henry VIII's marriage with Ann Boleyn and his break
with the Catholic Church.

In a climactic scene toward the end of the play, More's daughter
Margaret is given permission to see her father in prison if she will try
to persuade him to take the oath. Their conversation is a powerful lesson on the making of covenants and the taking of oaths:

Margaret: "God more regards the thoughts of the heart than the
words of the mouth. Or so you've always told me."

More: "Yes."

Margaret: "Then say the words of the oath and in your heart think
otherwise."

More: "What is an oath then but words we say to God? . . . When a
man takes an oath, Meg, he's holding his own self in his own hands.
Like water. [He cups his hands.] And if he opens his fingers then—he
needn't hope to find himself again. Some men aren't capable of this,
but I'd be loathe to think your father one of them."

In a very real sense we do what More described when we make
sacred covenants in the temple. We hold our eternal destiny in our
own hands. Most people don't flagrantly break their temple covenants
and fling the water of their souls away. Unworthiness usually comes in
more subtle ways. It slips through our fingers through our apathy or
our over-involvement in the things of the world.

As has been mentioned, often the payment of tithes and offerings
constitutes the commandment so many families do not keep. And of
course, if we cannot live this law we will never live the higher laws we
bind ourselves to practice during the endowment ceremony.

THE ISSUE WAS SIMPLE

Robert Bolt deeply admired Sir Thomas More. He wrote a lengthy
explanation of More as a preface to his play. In his descriptions, we
find other truths applicable to our own commitment to sacred oaths

made at holy altars: "A man takes an oath only when he wants to commit himself quite exceptionally to the statement, when he wants to make an identity between the truth of it and his own virtue; he offers himself as a guarantee. And it works. There is a special kind of shrug for a perjurer; we feel that the man has no self to commit, no guarantee to offer. . . .

"[More] was asked to retreat from that final area where he located his self. And there this supple, humorous, unassuming and sophisticated person set like metal, was overtaken by an absolutely primitive rigor, and could no more be budged than a cliff. . . .

"For him an oath was something perfectly specific; it was an *invitation to God, an invitation God would not refuse, to act as a witness, and to judge.* . . . So for More the issue was simple." (*A Man for All Seasons,* pp. xi-xii; emphasis added.)

So too, for us, must the issue be simple. A single covenant, when rightly perceived, removes hours of future decision-making and fortifies us against future temptation. We may not be perfect in obeying our covenants, but we must make a steady effort to be true. Nobody "lives up to his ideals," Heber J. Grant said, "but if we are striving, if we are working, if we are trying, to the best of our ability, to improve day by day, then we are in the line of our duty. If we are seeking to remedy our own defects, if we are so living that we can ask God for light, for knowledge, for intelligence, and above all for His spirit, that we may overcome our weaknesses, then, I can tell you, we are in the straight and narrow path that leads to life eternal; then we need have no fear." (*Conference Report,* April 1909, p. 111.) Brigham Young also taught this comforting doctrine: "No matter what the outward appearance is," he said, "if I can know of a truth that the hearts of the people are fully set to do the will of their Father in heaven, though they may falter and do a great many things through the weaknesses of human nature, yet, they will be saved." (*Journal of Discourses* 5:256.)

"SPEEDILY REPENT"

At all costs, we must not be apathetic to the temple or treat our covenants lightly. If we are now unworthy, we must not let years go by before we return. The Lord knew that some people would fail to maintain their temple worthiness through the temptations and weaknesses of human nature. But we are not so much condemned for our mistakes and sins as we are for our failure to cease doing them. In terms of temple covenants, the condemnation comes for not correcting our faults so that we can return to the temple. Worthiness and the desire to return to the temple are often the best signs we have that our repentance has been complete and is accepted by the Lord. Then we must forgive ourselves, continue with our lives, and remain temple worthy.

Even the dedicatory prayer of the Kirtland Temple refers to these things: "When thy people transgress, any of them, they may *speedily repent* and return unto thee, and find favor in thy sight, and be restored to the blessings which thou hast ordained to be poured out upon those who shall reverence thee in thy house." (D&C 109:21.) The invitation to come to the Lord's house is always extended. "I have set before thee an open door," Jesus said, "and no man can shut it." (Revelation 3:8.) Only our own refusal to enter that door will permanently keep us out of the Lord's kingdom.

CHAPTER 13

Crowning, Inspiring Privileges

In the temple, we make covenants with the Lord, and we are given laws and commandments by which to govern our lives. Unfortunately such words as *covenants, laws,* and *commandments* may not carry the most positive connotations in our minds. Sometimes we feel they are restrictive, limiting, authoritative, confining, restraining, or inhibiting. The Lord's attitude is much different. In the Doctrine and Covenants he explains that the "commandments" given to Joseph Smith "inspired" the Prophet. (D&C 20:7.) In section 51 the Lord gave the Saints the "*privilege* of organizing themselves according to [his] laws." (V. 15; emphasis added.) Later, in section 59, the Lord promises that the obedient will be "*crowned* with blessings from above, yea, and with commandments *not a few.*" (V. 4; emphasis added.)

Does our attitude toward commandments and laws encompass the words *inspiring, privilege, crowned,* or *blessing?* I doubt that many of us have prayed: "Lord, please 'crown' me with commandments and laws." Are we excited to receive "commandments not a few?" When we receive new commandments, are they always "inspiring"? But when rightly viewed, covenants, which always contain binding commitments, are a blessing. It is a privilege to receive them, and they do inspire us to a nobler life.

With this attitude, we find it easier to obey temple covenants. We are not so bothered, for instance, that we cannot wear the latest styles of shorts, dresses, or other clothing because we have made covenants regarding our temple garments. We are more focused on the inspiring, blessed, crowning privilege it is to wear them reverently that we may receive the specific promises the Lord grants us in return.

"Satisfactory Growth" in All Areas

When I was a boy I misbehaved. I seemed to disturb every class I attended. In Primary I was nicknamed the Holy Terror. No teachers wanted me in their classes, and I'm told there was a celebration when I finally graduated. I was not malicious or rebellious; I simply couldn't sit still. I felt restricted and confined, and I always had something I needed to say to my neighbor. I remember being hauled out of Sunday School class by a counselor in the bishopric and deposited in a chair next to my mother in the adult class, which she just happened to be teaching. The class was on parent-child relationships.

In school, things were not much better. I recently found some of my old elementary report cards in the basement. They told a tale I remember all too well. Every report card had a section called "Growth in Character and Citizenship." It was divided into six areas, each of which had a little check box in which the teacher indicated the student's progress. My report cards all looked basically the same: "1. Works Well with Others: Greater Growth Needed. 2. Plays Well with Others: Greater Growth Needed. 3. Shows Self-control: Greater Growth Needed. 4. Completes Work: Greater Growth Needed. 5. Is Thrifty with Time and Materials: Greater Growth Needed. 6. Assumes Responsibility toward School and Safety Rules: Greater Growth Needed."

Often the teacher would write some comments to the student's parents. My comments usually contained this sentence: "Michael needs to practice more self-control." My kindergarten teacher wrote: "Michael must be reminded of our rules quite often, thereby taking up more than his share of individual teacher-time. His attention span is short." Six months later, her final comment before promoting me to the first grade was: "Michael still must be reminded of rules quite often."

Time passed, but I didn't seem to change much. My third-grade teacher wrote: "Mike must learn to be more considerate of others. He is very impatient with written work—if he would relax and work slower, his papers would be much neater." Almost every report had a comment about my poor penmanship, which to this day hasn't improved. Another teacher's final comment was, "Encourage all his work habits." After checking the "Greater Growth Needed" boxes, another teacher wrote: "Mike still interrupts continually in class. I hope he will control this next year."

This continued right up until the eighth grade, when I began to get control of myself and my citizenship grades improved.

My fifth-grade report card stands out from all the others. In the "Growth in Character and Citizenship" section, my teacher, Mr. Burns, had boldly checked every single category in the "Satisfactory Growth" box. It was a perfect report card. In the area for the teacher's comments, Mr. Burns wrote: "Mike is a good boy in every respect. He studies hard, he plays hard—all in all I'm very proud of him. His improvement is in all areas, and I know he is aware of this growth and is trying harder. True, his writing isn't what it could be, but with constant effort and time, Mike will find growth and satisfaction in this area. Keep going, Mike!"

I will never forget Mr. Burns. I loved him. He was a boyhood hero. I would have done anything to please him, and I remember consciously trying to do anything that would win his approval. For Mr. Burns I would even sit still in class and not talk to my neighbor. My love for this teacher enabled me to keep all the rules, control my behavior, try my hardest to write neatly, and show "satisfactory growth" in all areas.

Love is the secret to obedience. It gives us the strength to keep our covenants and to try even harder when we fail. We obey God because we love him. We keep our temple covenants because we love him and know that our diligence in striving to live the kind of life we are taught in his house pleases him. He is our hero, and we want more than anything else to please him so that he can record "Satisfactory Growth" in all areas. Knowing that he is our Father helps the love to flow more purely. No wonder Satan is so eager to destroy the knowledge that every person on earth is a literal son or daughter of God.

"A THOUSAND TIMES MORE FAIR"

Sometimes we obey the rules, commandments, policies, or covenants of the Lord for reasons other than love. We obey out of fear, guilt, or a desire for reward. These attitudes bring obedience but not lasting obedience. In the scriptures, the covenant relationship of the Lord with his people is often compared to that of a bridegroom and his bride. This type of love is sweet; it seeks to please and focus on the beloved. It desires to make eternal covenants of lasting devotion. Love songs all over the world celebrate the eternal, unchanging power of love. Surely our love for the Bridegroom should be the same. In *The Merchant of Venice*, Shakespeare gives a beautiful description of the power of love. Portia, speaking to her beloved Bassanio, says:

> *You see me, Lord Bassanio, where I stand,*
> *Such as I am. Though for myself alone*
> *I would not be ambitious in my wish,*
> *To wish myself much better; yet for you*
> *I would be trebled twenty times myself—*
> *A thousand times more fair. . . .*
> *That only to stand high in your account,*
> *I might in virtues, beauties, livings, friends,*
> *Exceed account. But the full sum of me*
> *Is sum of something which, to term in gross,*
> *Is an unlessoned girl, unschooled, unpracticed,*
> *Happy in this, she is not yet so old*
> *But she may learn. Happier than this,*
> *She is not bred so dull but she can learn.*
> *Happiest of all is that her gentle spirit*
> *Commits herself to yours to be directed,*
> *As from her lord, her governor, her king.*
> *Myself and what is mine to you and yours*
> *Is now converted. But now I was the lord*
> *Of this fair mansion, master of my servants,*
> *Queen o'er myself. And even now, but now,*
> *This house, these servants, and this same myself*
> *Are yours, my lord.*
>
> (ACT III, SCENE II, LINES 150–173.)

This is the spirit of the temple. We give ourselves and all that we are freely at the altar, as Portia freely and joyfully gave her all to Bassanio. Like Portia, we wish we were a thousand times more righteous, more dedicated, more fit instruments in the Lord's hands. This devotion gives us the ability to keep our temple covenants to each other and to the Lord. It sanctifies the covenants and makes them holy.

In another beautiful scene from classical literature, Dante has Virgil respond to a command from Beatrice with the following words: "Thy command so pleases me that to obey it, were it already done, were slow to me." (*The Divine Comedy,* canto II, lines 78–80.) Knowing whose commands and laws we bind ourselves to obey, should any of us ever hesitate to respond quickly?

The scriptures present numerous examples of this beautiful attitude toward covenants and commandments from the Lord. Notice the sweetness contained in the following statements of men and women of the past. When the Lord called the boy Samuel, his response was, "Speak, for thy servant heareth." (1 Samuel 3:10.) When Mary was told she would bear the Redeemer of the world, her response to Gabriel showed her trusting love: "Behold the handmaid of the Lord; be it unto me according to thy word." (Luke 1:38.) When an angel asked Adam why he offered sacrifices to the Lord, he replied, "I know not, save the Lord commanded me." (Moses 5:6.) The Lord asked Isaiah, "Whom shall I send and who will go for us?" Isaiah replied, "Here am I; send me." (Isaiah 6:8.) On the road to Damascus, Paul asked, "Lord, what wilt thou have me to do?" (Acts 9:6.) Nephi's wonderful example of obedience is known by all: "I will go and do," he told his father. Then he went, "not knowing beforehand, the things which [he] should do." (1 Nephi 3:7; 4:6.) It should not be surprising that Nephi's last recorded words were "I must obey." (2 Nephi 33:15.) When Jesus said to Peter, "Launch out into the deep, and let down your nets," Peter responded, "Master, we have toiled all the night, and have taken nothing: nevertheless at thy word I will let down the net." (Luke 5:4–5.)

All of these examples are but reflections of the great example of Jesus himself. At the age of twelve, while teaching in the temple, he asked his mother: "How is it that ye sought me? Wist ye not that *I must be about my Father's business?*" (Luke 2:49; emphasis added.) But the ultimate expression of this wonderful attitude was displayed when the Father said: "Whom shall I send? And one answered like unto the Son of Man: Here am I, send me." (Abraham 3:27.) Later, as he knelt in Gethsemane, he verified his premortal willingness to atone when he said, "If it be possible, let this cup pass from me. Nevertheless, not as I will, but as thou wilt." (Matthew 26:39.)

Each of these examples shows an obedience born of love and trust. Most of these people did not always understand the full meaning or need of the commands, but they knew they loved the Lord, and his command was reason enough. Without hesitation they could bind themselves to obey. This is not blind obedience. We do not believe in blind obedience in this church, but we do believe in trust obedience. Experience will soon show that trust obedience always ends in enlightened obedience, as it did with each of the above individuals. As we contemplate the inspiring covenants and commandments of the temple, let us cultivate the attitudes of Portia, Virgil, the great men and women of the scriptures, and, above all, the example of our Lord and Savior, Jesus Christ.

PART 5

HOUSE OF GLORY

We praise Thee that our fathers, from last to first, from now, back to the beginning, can be united with us in indissoluble links, welded by the Holy Priesthood, and that as one great family united in Thee and cemented by Thy Power we shall together stand before Thee, and by the power of the atoning blood of Thy Son be delivered from all evil, be saved and sanctified, exalted and glorified.

(SALT LAKE TEMPLE DEDICATORY PRAYER.)

CHAPTER 14

The Parable of the Keys

The power of the temple in our own personal lives urges us to enter its doors. But there are other equally compelling reasons to enter the doors of the temple often—those relating to the dead. The temple ordinances never mean more to me than when I am participating in work for my own ancestors. The spirit of Elijah burns stronger and brighter and more clearly, illuminating the symbols of the temple and amplifying all temple blessings. I swim in the river more deeply, gain more knowledge and insight, feel greater serenity, am more certain of protection, desire to make a stronger commitment to my covenants, and am more attentive when I officiate for one of my own ancestors. The Lord's love seems to flow more softly and peacefully at these times. All that I learn is magnified, and the full power of the temple is realized. I am not suggesting that the temple will not bless in every way those who unselfishly officiate for the dead using the names the temple supplies. But a refinement of the Spirit and a fulness of joy is granted to those who take this additional and often time-consuming step in temple worship.

All the doctrines, principles, and ordinances of the gospel are inherently simple. We can all understand them and teach them to others if we will rely on the scriptures, the teachings of the Brethren, the whisperings of the Holy Ghost, and some good common sense. The temple is no different; its power is in its simplicity.

The Primary theme for 1993 centered on the temple. During that year I had the opportunity to speak to children about the Lord's house.

I shared with them the wonderfully descriptive passage from Ezekiel discussed earlier; then I told them a parable. I found that telling it was the best thing I could do to help children understand work for the dead. In its telling, I discovered that adults also related to it and grew in understanding. So much of what I would like to say about the temple as it relates to the living and the dead is contained in it.

The truth the parable attempts to amplify is stressed in section 128 of the Doctrine and Covenants. There Joseph Smith wrote: "My dearly beloved brethren and sisters, let me assure you that these are principles in relation to the dead and the living that cannot be lightly passed over, as pertaining to our salvation. For their salvation is necessary and essential to our salvation, as Paul says concerning the fathers—that they without us cannot be made perfect—neither can we without our dead be made perfect. . . . Neither can they nor we be made perfect without those who have died in the gospel also." (Vv. 15, 18.)

Notice that the "welding link" that perfects us is not only for those who died without the gospel but also for "those who have died *in the gospel.*" The whole human family must become a "whole and complete and perfect union." (D&C 128:18.) To that end I offer this parable.

THE PARABLE OF THE KEYS

Once there was a little boy and a little girl who loved Jesus very much, and he loved them. They were kind and always told the truth, and whatever Jesus wanted them to do they tried their best to do.

"You may come to my house," Jesus told them one day, "and there I will give you a gift."

They put on their best clothes, made sure they were clean, and went to Jesus' house.

It was a beautiful house, and it made them feel beautiful too, just to be inside it. They met Jesus, and he gave them his gift. It was a key— a *wonderful* key.

"Take care of this key," he said. "Put it next to your heart. Don't let it tarnish or get rusty. Always keep it with you. One day it will open a wonderful door. Whenever you wish, you may return to my house, but each time I will ask to see the key."

They promised him they would, and they went home.

They returned often to Jesus' house, and each time he asked if they still had the key. And they always did.

One day he asked if they would follow him. He led them to a hill covered with green grass and trees. On top of the hill was a mansion in the middle of a beautiful garden. Even in their dreams they had never imagined anything so magnificent.

"Who lives here?" they asked him.

"You may," he answered. "This is your eternal home. I've been building it for you. The key I gave you fits a lock in the front door. Now run up the path and put your key into the lock."

They ran up the hill and through the garden to the front door.

"If it's this beautiful on the outside," they said, "it must be even more wonderful inside!"

But when they reached the front door, they stopped. It was the strangest door they had ever seen. Instead of one lock, the door was covered with locks, hundreds of locks, thousands of locks. And they had only one key.

They put their key into one of the locks. It wouldn't fit. They put it into another. It didn't fit that one either. They tried many different locks. Finally they found the one that fit. They turned the key and the lock clicked. But the door wouldn't open.

They ran back to Jesus. "We cannot open the door," they said. "It is covered with locks, and we have only one key."

He smiled at them and said: "Do you think you will be happy living in your mansion all alone? Is there anyone you would like to live with you there?"

They thought for a while and then answered, "We would like our families to live with us."

"Go and find them," he said. "Invite them to my house, and I will give each one their very own key. Soon you will have many keys." They rushed out eagerly to find their families. They found their fathers and mothers, their brothers and sisters, and all their cousins and brought them to Jesus' house. Just as he had promised, he gave each one a key. When all had been given a key, together they returned to the great door of the mansion.

Now they had dozens of keys, but there were thousands of locks, and the door still wouldn't open. They needed more keys.

Once again they returned to Jesus. "We have brought our families," they said. "But the door still won't open."

"Do your parents have a mother and father and brothers and sisters?" He asked them. "Do you think they will be happy living in the beautiful mansion without them? If you look hard enough, you will find many, many people. Bring them all to my house, and I will give each one a key."

They looked very hard, just as Jesus had told them. They found mothers and fathers. They found brothers and sisters. They found grandmas and grandpas and great-great-grandmothers and great-great-great-grandfathers. They found aunts and uncles and nieces and nephews and cousins.

They found them in big cities. They found them in tiny villages. Some lived by the seashore. Some lived on the open prairie. Some lived near the mountains. Some lived far across the ocean. And some lived close, just over the next hill.

Some were blacksmiths and some were farmers. There were cobblers and tailors and fishermen. There were teachers and mechanics and shopkeepers.

Some were tall with strange-looking hats. Others were short and wore wooden shoes. They spoke different languages and came from many different countries.

They found some with long blond hair that hung far down their backs in braids. They found some with short red hair that stuck straight up and had to be hidden under a hat.

The boy and girl searched until they had found everybody and all their families.

They brought all the fathers and mothers, the brothers and sisters, the aunts and uncles, the nieces and nephews, the grandmothers and grandfathers to Jesus' house. Inside he gave each one his or her own key.

Soon all the families were gathered before the great door. There was a lock for every key. They turned the keys, but the door remained closed. There was one final lock, a great big one right in the middle of the door, and no one had its key.

The boy and girl returned to Jesus. "We have found all our families," they said. "But the door still won't open. We're missing a key and don't know where to find it."

Jesus smiled, put his arms around them, and gave each one a kiss. "I have the last key," he said, and he held it up. It was bright and shining and beautiful.

"This is the key of my atonement," he said. "Am I not a member of the family? Do you think you will be happy living in your mansion without me? Do you think I would be happy living without you? Now that you have found the whole family, all my brothers and sisters, all our Father's children, together we will enter our eternal home, for home will always be where families live and love together."

He took their hands, and the whole family opened the door, entered the mansion, and spent an eternity of happiness together.

"In my Father's house are many mansions," Jesus said. "I go to prepare a place for you. And if I go and prepare a place for you, I will come again, and receive you unto myself; that where I am, there ye may be also. And whither I go ye know, and *the way ye know*." (John 14:2–4; emphasis added.)

We enter temples to receive from God the key necessary to open the door to our eternal home. Once we have that key in our own possession, we hold it sacred, and a desire is born within our heart that all our family, all those we love, receive a key also. Our love begins to stretch and swell until it includes not only our children and grandchildren but also our ancestors back through generations. In the temple we are given the precious key that unlocks not only eternal joy but also greater temporal fulfillment and an invitation to help the Lord unlock salvation and eternal life for all his children. In what more fulfilling work could we be engaged? Do we think we will be happy living in our mansion all alone?

CHAPTER 15

"This Most Glorious of All Subjects"

In the Doctrine and Covenants the temple is called a "house of glory." It is worthy of that title for several reasons. We are assured that the Lord's "presence" is there "continually" and that his "glory may rest down upon [his] people." (D&C 109:12.) We also know that "the glory of God is intelligence, or, in other words, light and truth." (D&C 93:36.) The temple is a place where the Lord's intelligence flows into the Saints, but the temple is a house of glory for another equally significant reason—within its walls the most glorious work of the Restoration is performed.

If we were asked what the most glorious subject belonging to the gospel is, what would we answer? There are so many wonderful, edifying aspects of the gospel that it would be difficult to single out just one as the most glorious. However, the scriptures answer the question for us. They plainly teach that temple work, particularly that performed for the dead, is "this *most glorious* of all subjects belonging to the everlasting gospel." (D&C 128:17; emphasis added.) What is it about temple work that makes it deserving of such praise? Why is it so glorious? Why does it hold a so high a position in light of all the other wonderful works of the gospel? I will try to answer this by relating how it has become a source of glory in my life and that of my family.

"REMEMBER ME"

When I was young, I read the stories of my Waldensian ancestors, whose beliefs brought upon their heads centuries of persecution. They lived in the Piedmont valleys of the Alps, where they could find a measure of protection from the anger of religious prejudice. There they tried to practice their faith according to the simple truths of the Bible. My third great-grandmother was, at the time, a fourteen-year-old French Waldensian named Pauline Combe, the daughter of Jean Combe. This is her story as it was penned by her daughter, my second great-grandmother Madeleine Malan: "Our ancestors were descendants of the Waldenses. . . . They adhered strictly to the Old and New Testaments. They held that the Holy Scriptures are the only source of faith and religion.

"When our mother Pauline Combe was near fifteen years of age in the spring of the year 1820, she went with her father down into the plains of Piedmont to take charge of a large cocoonery; each had a cot in the large spacious hall where they were tending the silk worms. One day, about a week or so before the season was ended, she had been reading about the life of Christ and his apostles; and the gospel as taught by them.

"At night, after retiring, she lay there pondering upon what she had been reading and wishing that she had been living in those days. The whole room became as light as noonday. She arose in sitting posture and a heavenly influence pervaded the room. She began singing a sacred hymn, when twelve personages dressed in white robes appeared and formed in a semicircle by her cot and joined in the singing, and at its conclusion they and the light departed. When she returned home, and related the vision to her mother, she in turn beside other remarks, read the 17th and 18th verses of the second chapter of Acts.

"Our grandfather Jean Combe was a religious man and went regularly to church hungering for the 'bread of life,' to be spiritually fed, but came away unsatisfied and would sometimes comment on the difference of the teaching of the day to those of the Savior and his apostles.

"When he was on his death bed, our sister Mary was sitting in the room and he said to her 'The old folks may not, but the young will see the day when the gospel shall be restored in its purity and powers; and in that day, Mary, *remember me!*'" (From the author's copy of the original document.)

Jean Combe, like his fathers before him, died without the saving ordinances of the gospel, without baptism, the gift of the Holy Ghost, the endowment, or being sealed to his eternal family. His fathers missed the great blessings of the priesthood by many years. He missed them by only a few. Shortly after Jean Combe's death, Lorenzo Snow and several other elders came to the shores of Italy. They were directed by the Spirit to the valleys of the Alps, to the village where Pauline's family lived. After hearing the truths of the restored gospel, they were the first family to join the Church in Italy.

Jean's last words have always been to me the call of all my ancestors down through the ages, reaching through the veil, asking to be remembered. If Jean Combe's family and his forebears were your ancestors, would it not be a glorious thing to enter a temple and say, in essence, to them: "Here are my eyes; together we will look upon the beauty of the Lord's house. Here are my ears; let us hear the words of eternal life. Here are my lips; we will make sacred covenants. Here are my hands; together we will receive the gifts of life everlasting. Here are my knees; kneel with me at the altars of salvation, there to become one with all those we both love. *I will remember you.*" Nothing I have ever done is more glorious.

"I AM SATISFIED"

In Lancashire, England, in the 1850s lived a woman named Ann Massey Clegg. She was a widow of delicate health, rearing five children of her own and four of her husband's from a previous marriage. Every morning Ann watched her five-year-old son, Thomas, take his sisters' hands, walk to the cotton mill, and "work a 12 hour day in a dingy, poor ventilated room breathing into his lungs the lint from the cotton." They subsisted on "a little weak tea with a bun or a little cake of oatmeal mush in the bottom of a teacup." Life was bitter and hard. Ann hoped and prayed for better days.

Ann heard the message of the Restoration and joined the Church. Persecution followed. A mob dropped a bomb down her chimney, burning two of her children. Ann knew she had to find a better life for them. Through faith and prayer an opportunity came. A wealthy squire offered to pay the passage of five families to Zion, and Ann's was chosen. In spite of failing health, fearing that another opportunity might never come, she undertook the long journey.

Weeks on the ocean and the overland trip to Nebraska took their toll. She became unable to walk, and her children placed her on a bed in the wagon. Before long she was too weak to lift her head, but she clung to life until she could see her children safe in Zion. When they reached Emigration Canyon, Thomas raised his mother's head so she could view the wonderful sight. She gazed at it in silence and then whispered, "I am satisfied."

Ann never regained her health and died a few weeks later. She died without the blessings of the holy endowment and without the sealing blessings of an eternal family. She was buried in an unmarked grave in City Cemetery. Generations later, grateful descendants placed over her grave a stone monument. It was inscribed, "I am satisfied." (History written by Beatrice Edwards Sorenson.)

Ann Massey Clegg is my wife's great-great-grandmother. If she were your ancestor, would it not be a glorious thing to enter a temple, perform for her the ordinances of eternal life, and say to her, "Here are my eyes; together we will look upon the beauty of the Lord's house. Here are my ears; let us hear the words of eternal life. Here are my lips; we will make sacred covenants. Here are my hands; together we will receive the gifts of life everlasting. Here are my knees; kneel with me at the altars of salvation, there to become one with all those we both love. *I will remember you.*"

"I Would Like to Come Together Again for Eternal Life"

In the early 1600s in the tiny village of Hirzel, Canton Zurich, Switzerland, lived the family of Hans Landis. They owned dairy cows and should have lived simple lives, but this was not their fate. Hans Landis was a Mennonite preacher whose faith was not acceptable to church or state authorities. After years of opposition, hiding, and imprisonment, Hans was beheaded in a public square in Zurich in 1614. The authorities ordered that his wife, Margaretha Hochstrasser, "be taken to the Spital in the death room and bound and only the most necessary care given. No one will be allowed to speak to her or

enter the room, in hope she may in this wise be listening and con-
verted." (From the author's copy of an original document.)

The family's property was confiscated and the children scattered.
Their son Felix was starved to death in prison. Their daughter Verena
died under house arrest. Another son, Hans, named for his father, was
sent to prison, where he wrote the following letter that is still preserved
in the archives of Zurich: "I send to you my dear wife greetings and all
of you in the name of the Lord and Savior. I am letting you know how
I am, that I am well and pray by the grace of God the Almighty, he may
keep myself and all of you in his truth. I want to let you know that the
men have already returned twice since I've been imprisoned here, and
they will return to me; therefore, pray to God earnestly for us that he
may watch over us and give us the will to speak and be silent when
necessary.

"Again, I ask you, dear mother, that you may diligently watch over
the children and admonish them to pray and to read and be God fearing, as you well know what we talked about when I was with you.
Concerning the children, I exhort you to be very obedient; if the Lord
makes me free again I will be able to further show you truly how to
carry out his commanded word throughout the land, with your whole
will, and within the meaning of Christ's will; nothing else should be
heeded than God and the word of His basic commands, and this alone
should be truly praised by us.

"Written by myself, Hans Landis, imprisoned in Ottenbach, 1637."
(From the author's copy of the original document.)

I do not know what became of the writer of this letter. A little time
later he wrote again to his wife: "I don't know whether or not I will be
coming to you, I entrust myself to the commands of the loving God,
in his shelter and protection truly, amen. . . . *I would like to come
together again for eternal life,* if we diligently live and abide by his will.
For this, my children be very desirous and have much love for each
other, I ask you truly to do this with your entire will. If you do so, it
would bring you *a great treasure* after this time in eternal life. . . . I
resign myself to what the Lord has sent me." (From the author's copy
of original manuscript)

Hans Landis's children's names were found on a list of exiles to

France not long after the last letter was written. The list indicates that the parents of the children were dead. I assume they died in Switzerland as a result of persecution. Hans Landis, who wrote these letters, is one of my ancestors. Some of his grandchildren finally found peace in William Penn's new state, Pennsylvania. Since the letters are preserved in the Zurich archives, they may never have been sent.

The courage of this family has been an inspiration to me and my children. They were true to the knowledge they possessed but died without the saving ordinances of the gospel. In life they were scattered, but through the ordinances of the Lord's house they have "come together again for eternal life" and "found a great treasure."

If the Landis family were your ancestors, would it not be a glorious thing to enter a temple and say to them: "Here are my eyes; together we will look upon the beauty of the Lord's house. Here are my ears; let us hear the words of eternal life. Here are my lips; we will make sacred covenants. Here are my hands; together we will receive the gifts of life everlasting. Here are my knees; kneel with me at the altars of salvation, there to become one with all those we both love. *I will remember you.*"

We must never forget that we do the work for real people who had joys and sorrows just as we do. They faced the challenges of their lives with courage and dignity. They loved their families and made sacrifices for their God. We do not do the work for names but for lives, and in doing it our souls are bound to them and theirs to ours. That is why it is so glorious.

They are dead to this world but are alive in the world of spirits, alive to God, and alive in our hearts. "The spirits of the just," Joseph Smith taught, "are . . . enveloped in flaming fire, . . . *are not far from us,* and know and understand our thoughts, feelings, and motions." (*Teachings of the Prophet Joseph Smith,* p. 326; emphasis added.) In the temple, where the veil is thinnest, the welding link of love is forged.

President Joseph F. Smith believed that the spirits of the dead were deeply committed and desirous for the welfare of their descendants. He wrote: "I claim that we live in their presence, they see us, they are solicitous for our welfare, they love us now more than ever. . . . They see the temptations and the evils that beset us in life, and the proneness of mortal beings to yield to temptation and to wrong doing; hence their solicitude for us and their love for us and their desire for our well being must be greater than that which we feel for ourselves. . . . If we can see, by the enlightening influence of the Spirit of God and through the words that have been spoken by the holy prophets of God beyond the veil that separates us from the spirit world, surely those who have passed beyond can see more clearly through the veil back here to us than it is possible for us to see to them from our sphere of action. . . . we are not separated from them. . . . We cannot forget them; we do not cease to love them; we always hold them in our hearts, in memory, and thus we are associated and united to them by ties that we cannot break, that we cannot dissolve, or free ourselves from." (*Gospel Doctrine,* pp. 430–31.)

THOSE IN DARKNESS

Even if our ancestors' lives were not noble and courageous, even if they made less than desirable choices, the work we perform is still meaningful and essential. President Brigham Young told the Saints, "Go and perform the ordinances of the house of God for those who have passed their probation without the Gospel, and *for all who will receive any kind of salvation; bring them up to inherit the celestial, terrestrial, and telestial kingdoms.*" (*Discourses of Brigham Young,* pp. 624–25; emphasis added.)

In his wonderful vision of the redemption of the dead, now recorded in section 138 of the Doctrine and Covenants, President Joseph F. Smith spoke of those spirits who were in "darkness." These he described as "the wicked, . . . the ungodly and the unrepentant who had defiled themselves while in the flesh . . . the rebellious who rejected the testimonies and the warnings of the ancient prophets . . . and the disobedient." (Vv. 20–29.)

Among these Jesus did not go in person, but he organized his forces and sent them to those "in darkness, even to *all* the spirits of men." (V. 30; emphasis added.) His forces carried "the message of redemption unto *all* the dead, unto whom he [Jesus] could not go personally, because of their rebellion and transgression." (V. 37; emphasis added.) The gospel was proclaimed to *all* who would repent, both "those who had died in their sins, without a knowledge of the truth, or in transgression, having rejected the prophets." (Vv. 31–32; emphasis added.) Both groups "were taught faith in God, repentance from sin, *vicarious baptism* for the remission of sins, the gift of the Holy Ghost by the laying on of hands, and all other principles of the gospel that were necessary for them to know. . . . And so it was made known among the dead, both *small and great,* the *unrighteous as well as the faithful,* that redemption had been wrought through the sacrifice of the Son of God upon the cross." (Vv. 33–35; emphasis added. See also D&C 76:71–74.)

Joseph F. Smith saw that "the faithful elders of this dispensation" continued to preach "the gospel of repentance and redemption through the sacrifice of the Only Begotten Son of God, among those who are in *darkness and under the bondage of sin* in the great world of the spirits of the dead." (V. 57; emphasis added.) We have already seen that those who are in "darkness" are the "wicked, rebellious, disobedient, unrepentant" souls who "defiled themselves" and "rejected the testimonies and the warnings of the ancient prophets." (Vv. 20–21.)

President Smith saw that "the dead who repent [referring to those in darkness] will be *redeemed, through obedience to the ordinances of the house of God,* and after they have paid the penalty of their transgressions, and are washed clean, shall receive a reward according to their works, *for they are heirs of salvation."* (Vv. 58–59; emphasis added. See also D&C 76:88.) Earlier in his life President Smith spoke of these same principles. "Here will come in the principles of baptism for the dead," he said, "and of proxy and heirships, as revealed through the prophet Joseph Smith, that *they may receive a salvation and an exaltation, I will not say a fullness of blessing and glory, but a reward according to their merits* and the righteousness and mercy of God, even as it will be with you and with me." (*Gospel Doctrine,* p. 477; emphasis added.)

The Lord has taken the burden of judgment from our shoulders. We do not need to wonder which of our ancestors is in need of temple ordinances. We will perform them for all we find. They all need them—those who dwell in darkness for rebellion as well as the sincere, noble souls who lived up to the best light they had. We must help

release them from their "bondage" and "captivity," through "the ordinances of the house of God," that they may receive "*a* salvation and *an*
exaltation." The rest we will leave with the Lord. He alone can righ-
teously judge and assign eternal rewards. He will deal with all the dead
as Mormon told us God would deal with the fallen Nephites: "The
Father, yea the Eternal Father of heaven, knoweth your state; and he
doeth with you according to his justice and mercy." (Mormon 6:22.)

CHAPTER 16

Elijah Will Come

The altars of the temple are places of offering and sacrifice. There we offer our Father in Heaven our hearts and our lives. There we are taught how to "come unto Christ . . . and offer [our] whole souls as an offering unto him" (Omni 1:26), but we also offer him "the greatest selfless act of Christian service that we can perform in this mortal life," that of work for the dead. (Gordon B. Hinckley, Dedication Address, Taiwan Temple.)

The major work of this dispensation and the whole thrust of the Restoration centers on those offerings. Everything we do in the Church focuses on and moves us toward the altars of the temple. If we do not kneel at those altars for ourselves and our dead and remain true to the covenants and principles we are taught, the work of the Church in our lives has largely been frustrated. We can illustrate this truth by an appeal to the scriptures. There, in the first pages of the Bible, we find two beautifully symbolic images of the temple.

In Genesis 28 is recorded one of the first descriptions of a temple. There was no building, just a hilltop, but the sacred event that took place there provides us with marvelous insight about the importance of the temple.

While traveling to Haran, Jacob had a dream wherein he beheld "a *ladder set up on the earth,* and the top of it reached to heaven: and behold the angels of God ascending and descending on it. And, behold, the Lord stood above it." (Vv. 12–13; emphasis added.) Here the word *ladder* is better translated as "stairway." (See *The New Strong's*

Exhaustive Concordance of the Bible.) Here is one of the finest descriptions of a temple in scripture. A temple is a stairway set up on earth whose top reaches to heaven. It is the meeting place of heaven and earth, a place where the dead and the living communicate with one another and where the Spirit teaches beautiful lessons. It is a place where those who have preceded us in the spirit world descend to us while we ascend to them.

The Lord and Jacob exchanged covenants, just as we do now in our modern temples. As part of his covenant, the Lord promised Jacob: "I am with thee, and will keep thee in all places whither thou goest. . . . I will not leave thee, until I have done that which I have spoken to thee of." (V. 15.) This promised companionship and protection is a major blessing of faithful temple worship, as discussed earlier.

In return, "Jacob vowed a vow, saying, If God will be with me, and will keep me in this way that I go . . . then shall the Lord be my God." Part of his vow was a promise to "give the tenth" of all he had to the Lord. (Vv. 20–22.)

When Jacob awoke from his dream, he concluded, "Surely the Lord is in this place; and I knew it not. . . . This is none other but the house of God, and this is the *gate of heaven.*" (Vv. 16–17; emphasis added.) Above the stairway and through the gate, the Lord stood, waiting to receive Jacob into his kingdom, but first the stairway had to be climbed and the gate passed.

I love these descriptions of the temple. They are beautiful and instructive in their simplicity. The temple is a stairway. We must climb it in order to reach our Father in Heaven. Everything in the Church funnels us toward the stairway and encourages us to climb. The climb will require effort, but even the effort is rewarding. The temple is also a gate. We must pass through it or forever remain outside the kingdom of God. There is simply no other way for the living or the dead to return to and dwell in the presence of God. In this dispensation, the Lord extends the glorious invitation of taking our ancestors by the hand and climbing with them up the stairway and through the gate. For this effort we were chosen and elected. To fulfill this promise the priesthood was restored. From first to last, this was the central thrust of the Restoration.

THE BEGINNING AND END OF THE GOSPEL

The angelic messengers who returned to restore the priesthood keys knew the stairway and gate the children of God had to climb and pass through before they could enjoy eternal life. Each messenger had firmly in mind the culmination to which each key would lead. The Doctrine and Covenants begins and ends with temple work. Elder John A. Widtsoe taught: "Almost the first words of the Lord to the Prophet Joseph Smith, when as a boy he was called to restore the Gospel of Jesus Christ, dealt with [temple work]; and almost the last words spoken by God to the Prophet before the Prophet's death, as far as we can tell, dealt with the same subject." ("Temple Worship," p. 50.)

Section 2 of the Doctrine and Covenants was given early in the Restoration by Moroni, on September 21, 1823. It is the first recorded revelation given in this dispensation and the only statement by Moroni to Joseph Smith given on the night of his first visit that was recorded in the Doctrine and Covenants. Malachi's prophecy that Elijah would come to "plant in the hearts of the children the promises made to the fathers" and that "the hearts of the children shall turn to their fathers" was also the first prophecy Moroni quoted to Joseph Smith. (V. 2; see Malachi 4:6.) Elder Widtsoe's testimony that "the beginning and the end of the Gospel is written, from one point of view, in Section 2 of the Book of Doctrine and Covenants" further amplifies the importance of this tiny section in the grand unrolling of the Restoration. ("Temple Worship," p. 64.)

PROMISES MADE TO THE FATHERS

The word *fathers* can be interpreted to mean our own individual fathers or the great patriarchal fathers Abraham, Isaac, and Jacob. This second meaning is clarified in section 27, where, speaking of the restoration of priesthood keys, the Lord calls Joseph, Jacob, Isaac, and Abraham *"your fathers, by whom the promises remain."* (V. 10; emphasis added.) We are involved in promises made to both individual and patriarchal fathers.

INDIVIDUAL FATHERS—HELP FROM BEYOND THE VEIL

In exchange for the gift of life and other blessings, we promised to provide our "fathers" with the ordinances of eternal life. They are counting on that promise and will do all they can to help us fulfill it, as will the Lord. The help may extend even so far as our own conversions. Often when I am on a speaking assignment, I ask all the converts in a congregation to stand. I then ask all who are the only Church member in their family to remain standing. Remarkably, in every case almost all remain standing. People tend to join the Church one or two in a family.

Elder Melvin J. Ballard reflected on this truth and received an answer to explain it. He taught: "Why is it that sometimes only one of a city or household receives the Gospel? It was made known to me that it is because the righteous dead who have received the Gospel in the spirit world are exercising themselves, and in answers to their prayers elders of the Church are sent to the homes of their posterity . . . , and that descendant in the flesh is then privileged to do the work for his dead kindred. I want to say to you that it is with greater intensity that the hearts of the fathers and mothers in the spirit world are turned to their children now in the flesh than that our hearts are turned to them." (Melvin J. Ballard, *Crusader for Righteousness,* p. 219.)

We often wonder if our ancestors will accept the gospel. Ironically, in many instances, they accepted it before we did. Their prayers and faithfulness have brought the gospel into our lives instead of the other way around. Officiating in the temple for them is a deep expression of our gratitude and helps bind us to them.

If we are in tune, they will also help us as we try to locate the documents that record their names. As Elder Ballard said: "They know where their records are, and . . . the spirit and influence of your dead will guide those who are interested in finding those records. . . . If there is anywhere on the earth anything concerning them, you will find it. . . . If we have done our best and have searched and have discovered all that is available, then the day will come when God will open and part the veil, and the records . . . will be revealed. (Bryant S. Hinckley, *Sermons and Missionary Services of Melvin Joseph Ballard,* p. 230.)

Recently in general conference, Elder David B. Haight gave an added witness to the truths taught by Elder Ballard: "I believe that when you diligently seek after your ancestors—in faith—needed information will come to you *even when no mortal records of their lives are available.*" (*Ensign,* May 1993, p. 25; emphasis added.)

"SOME KIND ANGEL"

May I add my own testimony to the willingness of our ancestors to help us keep our individual promises to them. Once in frustration and despair I sat in the Church's Family History Library about to give up a twenty-five-year search for a certain ancestor. The ancestor I sought was known by my grandmother, a fourth-generation member of the Church, who could have called him on the telephone and asked him who his parents were. Now both he and my grandmother were dead, and I felt the sorrow of lost opportunities.

A warning given in the *Millennial Star* in 1853 was certainly true for our family. It said, "If you neglect the opportunities you now have of securing this information, you will see the time when you will perhaps seek for it, but not be able to find it, until you have so far paid the debt of your neglect, that some kind angel from the spirit world will be justified in bringing to you the necessary intelligence." (*Millennial Star,* August 6, 1853, p. 522.) As I sat in the library that day, I knew I needed "some kind angel."

"Grandmother," I said in my heart, "you could have found the answer so easily, and now it's too late. Help me, now, to find something, any record at all, that can provide a clue. Help me find him, not only for his sake but also for all the generations that wait behind him."

I decided to make one last effort by searching through a large number of microfilms. The task would have taken me hours. It was a long shot, but the only one I had. On my way to get them, I walked by some books, and my attention was drawn to a set of twenty volumes of Canadian marriages. On a whim, I picked one up and searched it. It contained nothing of interest. I searched a second and a third. Still I found nothing. I thought, "This is fruitless" and decided to stop the search, but I had the fourth volume in my hand already. "I'll search this," I thought, "and then quit."

I opened the pages. There was the marriage of my ancestor, complete with his parents and his wife's parents and their places of birth. Overcome with emotion, I shut the book, hugged it, sat on the floor, and wept. Then I thanked my grandmother, who I know guided me to the only record in the library where critical information on my ancestor could be found.

Within a few months the line was extended nine generations. The story of Hans Landis that I related earlier was a result of that afternoon's discovery in the library. Since that time, more than two thousand names have been submitted for temple work as a result of that experience. I know we will receive help in fulfilling our promises if we allow them to be "planted" and take root in our hearts.

I have sensed from time to time, as I ponder the story of Moroni's visit and read the words he first quoted to Joseph Smith, the joy of my own people behind the veil as the first step that would lead to their salvation was taught to a boy prophet in the upstairs room of a log cabin. We, too, can feel that joy, and the greater joy that will come one day as we meet again with our "fathers," having fulfilled our promises to them.

A blessing that has produced some of the greatest joy and anticipation in my own life is a promise in my patriarchal blessing that says I and my posterity may have the privilege of fulfilling the promises made to our forefathers. Then, after the promises are fulfilled, we may meet with them in the Resurrection with love, fellowship, and great rejoicing together.

PATRIARCHAL FATHERS—ALL THE FAMILIES OF THE EARTH

Our other "fathers" are Abraham, Isaac, and Jacob. They were promised that their "seed" would bless "all the families of the earth . . . with the blessings of the Gospel, which are the blessings of salvation, even of life eternal." (Abraham 2:11.) Over and over in the scriptures we are reminded that the Abrahamic covenant ensured that all the families of all nations would receive blessings through the posterity of Abraham, Isaac, and Jacob. (See Genesis 12:3; 17:4; 18:18; 22:18; 26:4; 28:14.)

Nephi taught his brothers when this covenant promise would find fulfillment: "Our father hath not spoken of our seed alone, but also of all the house of Israel, pointing to the covenant which should be fulfilled *in the latter days;* which covenant the Lord made to our father Abraham, saying: In thy seed shall all the kindreds of the earth be blessed." (1 Nephi 15:18; emphasis added.) This promise is fulfilled when we proclaim the gospel in all nations, but to a much larger extent it is fulfilled when Abraham's seed rise up, go into the temples, and provide the redeeming ordinances of the gospel that bring the "blessings of salvation, even of life eternal" for "all the *families* of the earth." (Abraham 2:11; emphasis added.) Temple work is essentially done in behalf of families. In the latter days, the need and the desire to provide all the blessings of the gospel for all generations would be planted in the hearts of the children of Abraham. In the temples, that promise would be fulfilled.

That is one reason the declaring of our lineages in our patriarchal blessings is so critically important. These blessings are called "patriarchal" because they are given to us by our stake patriarchs, but they are also called "patriarchal" because in them the promises and responsibilities of the great patriarchs are made manifest in our lives and are pronounced upon our heads.

Each blessing is an individual call to fulfill the promise to Abraham that his seed would bless the families of the earth. From one point of view, the promises made to the fathers are planted in our hearts when a patriarch's hands are laid upon our heads and our lineage is declared.

THE ROLE OF A GATHERING

All these things Moroni knew as he spoke to Joseph Smith in 1823. He knew to what culmination the restoration of the priesthood would lead, and he also knew the role the Book of Mormon would play in the fulfillment of the Abrahamic promises and in the coming work of the temples. The Book of Mormon was the voice of the Good Shepherd, and his sheep would hear his voice in its pages. "The scriptures shall be given," the Lord told Joseph Smith, "even as they are in mine own bosom, to the salvation of mine own elect; for they will *hear my voice,* and shall see me, and shall not be asleep, and shall abide the day of my coming." (D&C 35:20–21; emphasis added.) The voice of the Savior in the Book of Mormon would be the key to the "gathering" of the Saints presented to the world by the work of dedicated missionaries. But why gather the Saints?

Joseph Smith taught that there is only one purpose for a gathering—to build temples. "It is for the same purpose that God gathers together His people in the last days," he said, "to build unto the Lord a house to prepare them for the ordinances and endowments, washings and anointings, etc. . . . What was the object of gathering the Jews or the people of God in any age of the world? . . . The main object was to build unto the Lord a house whereby He could reveal unto His people the ordinances of His house and the glories of His kingdom, and teach the people the way of salvation." (*History of the Church* 5:423–24.) In the early days of the Church, all were encouraged to gather to a central spot, for there were few members and fewer temples. Now we have many members and many stakes. The nature of the gathering has not changed. We still gather around temples, or we gather so that more temples may be built. One day we hope to have many more temples in many more states and countries.

David, also, testified of this grand purpose of a gathering when he wrote, "O send out thy light and thy truth: let them lead me; let them bring me unto thy holy hill, and to thy tabernacles. Then will I go unto the altar of God, unto God my exceeding joy." (Psalm 43:3–4.) The Church sends the light of the gospel into the world and invites all to the Lord's house. Every missionary knows the goal he or she wishes new converts to reach. I always felt a great sense of relief when those I had taught and saw baptized finally reached the temple. I felt they had been gathered into the Lord's secure granary.

Moses bore his witness to the purpose of gathering in a song he wrote after the freeing of Israel from Egypt. He clearly taught that the Lord had "purchased" Israel and brought them into the promised land, and he prayed, "Plant them in the mountain of thine inheritance, in the place, O Lord, which thou hast made for thee to dwell in, in the Sanctuary, O Lord, which thy hands have established." (Exodus 15:17.)

In the Doctrine and Covenants we learn that the gathering of the

Saints and the building of Zion begins at the temple: "The city New Jerusalem shall be built by the gathering of the saints, beginning at this place, *even the place of the temple.*" (D&C 84:4; emphasis added.)

When persecutions in Jackson County forced the Saints to move to other counties, the Lord still emphasized the need to gather in order to build a temple: "The gathering together upon the land of Zion, and upon her stakes," the Lord told the Saints as they first began to build up Far West, "may be for a defense and for a refuge from the storm, and from wrath. . . . Therefore, I command you to build a house unto me, for the *gathering* together of my saints that they may worship me." (D&C 115:6–8; emphasis added.) Not surprisingly, everywhere the early Saints traveled, whether to Ohio, Missouri, Illinois, or Utah, one of the first things they did was to dedicate a spot for the Lord's house. It was the standard around which they would gather.

CHAPTER 17

An Acceptable Offering

Moroni promised Joseph Smith that the priesthood would be "revealed." This meant at least two things: (1) Its power and authority would be restored to the earth, and (2) its purpose would be made known to all who bore it faithfully. It is the second of these two purposes that especially bears on our present topic.

Not long after Moroni's promise, John the Baptist returned, bringing the first restoration of priesthood powers. With his mind centered on the temple, John the Baptist laid his hands on Joseph Smith and Oliver Cowdery, promising that the priesthood would "never be taken again from the earth, *until* the sons of Levi do offer again an offering unto the Lord in righteousness." (D&C 13:1; emphasis added.) John was quoting Malachi, the same prophet Moroni first quoted to Joseph Smith in 1823.

In Malachi, the prophecy reads a little differently. There "until" is replaced with "that": "He shall purify the Sons of Levi, and purge them as gold and silver, *that* they may offer unto the Lord an offering in righteousness." (Malachi 3:3; emphasis added.) That same reading is given in Doctrine and Covenants 128:24 and also in Oliver Cowdery's description of the coming of John the Baptist in the footnote on page 59 of the Pearl of Great Price. Oliver recorded that John the Baptist promised, "This priesthood and authority . . . shall remain upon earth, *that* the Sons of Levi may yet offer an offering unto the Lord in righteousness."

Both words are important and true. We need not decide if one is more correct than the other. The priesthood was restored "that" the offering could be made. In other words, without it the offering could not be made. It was also restored "until" the offering was made. In other words, the priesthood would never be taken from the earth. That was a tremendous promise! As Moroni promised, the priesthood was being revealed by being restored, and its purpose was also being revealed—an offering had to be made. Obviously the offering is so important that no opposition will stop it. That is by the firm decree of the Lord himself. We also learn that the priesthood bearers must be "purged and purified" or made clean in order to make the offering.

Who are the sons of Levi? What offering will they make? Why is that offering so critical that the priesthood will not be taken from the earth? Why is it so important that the priesthood itself was restored to allow the offering to be accomplished? What do purging and purifying have to do with the offering? Let us try to answer these questions by an appeal to the scriptures.

THE SONS OF LEVI

In biblical times the sons of Levi were "appointed unto all manner of service of the tabernacle of the house of God." (1 Chronicles 6:48.) They "set forward the work of the house of the Lord." (1 Chronicles 23:4.)

Their "office was to wait on the sons of Aaron for the service of the house of the Lord, in the courts, and in the chambers, and in the purifying of all holy things." They kept "the charge of the tabernacle of the congregation, and the charge of the holy place." (1 Chronicles 23:1, 28, 32.) In other words, the sons of Levi were essentially the ancient temple ordinance workers.

As the Restoration proceeded, more information was revealed and more keys were restored concerning the offering spoken of by John the Baptist. On September 22 and 23, 1832, the anniversary of Moroni's visit, a great revelation was given on the priesthood. In this revelation the words of Malachi's and John the Baptist's prophecies were repeated, but with different and added words that amplified and gave further clarification about the necessary offering: "The *sons of Moses* and also the *sons of Aaron* shall offer an *acceptable* offering and sacrifice *in the house of the Lord.*" (D&C 84:31; emphasis added.)

Sons of Moses hold the Melchizedek priesthood; sons of Aaron hold the Aaronic. Moses and Aaron were both from the tribe of Levi. John the Baptist's promise refers to both priesthoods. We further learn that the offering will be made in "the house of the Lord." That helps explain why the sons of Levi must be purged and purified. One must be clean and worthy both to enter the temple and also to exercise priesthood authority.

It is not surprising that an "offering and sacrifice" should be accomplished in the temple. Offerings and sacrifices were done anciently at altars, and the altars of the temple stand at the center of all we do in the house of the Lord.

The Lord adds the word *acceptable* to the offering. When it is made, it will be made in such a manner that the Lord can receive it. The word becomes critically important later in understanding the exact nature of the offering.

KEYS AND TEMPLES

The progress of the Restoration continued. The Kirtland Temple was built, and important keys were there restored. The major themes of the priesthood were there emphasized by angelic messengers. "Moses appeared . . . and committed . . . the keys of the *gathering* of Israel from the four parts of the earth." The promise of Abraham was reiterated as "Elias appeared, and committed the dispensation of the gospel of Abraham, saying that in us and our seed *all generations* after us should be blessed." Elijah then returned to complete the necessary authority to "turn the hearts of the fathers to the children, and the children to the fathers." (D&C 110:11, 12, 15; emphasis added.) The gathering, the Abrahamic covenant, and the turning of hearts are all inseparably connected with temples. The proper authority was now in place, and the offering could now be made.

The Saints moved on to Nauvoo and once again were given the command to build a temple. They had learned in Missouri the importance of responding to that command. Their failure to do so was a major factor in their expulsion from Jackson County. (See

D&C 97; 101:43–54.) They had learned in Kirtland that when the Lord gave a command to build a temple and the Saints did not immediately respond, they had "sinned a very grievous sin," which the Lord compared to "walking in darkness at noon-day." (D&C 95:6.)

Now in Nauvoo the Lord revealed the redeeming work for the dead and pressed upon the Saints the necessity of completing a temple in order to begin this great work in a place sacred enough for its importance. With the command to build his house, the Lord added a sobering warning: "I command you, *all ye my saints,* to build a house unto me; and I grant unto you a sufficient time to build a house unto me; . . . and if you do not these things at the end of the appointment *ye shall be rejected as a church,* with your dead, saith the Lord your God." (D&C 124:31–32.)

Notwithstanding all the other works of the Church and the priesthood, the failure to construct a temple (where the Lord could "restore again . . . the fulness of the priesthood" [D&C 124:28] and where the offering could be made) would result in the *rejection* of the Church. In the minutes of the October 1841 conference, the Lord also instructed the Saints not to hold another conference until it could be held in the temple. Apparently, the Lord felt there was no need for further instructions until the most critical one of all was commenced. (*History of the Church* 4:426.)

A BOOK TO BE LAID ON THE ALTAR

The groundwork was now laid for the critical offering to be made, and it was looked forward to by all angelic messengers who had returned to earth to restore priesthood keys and authorities. However, Satan was not idle. Joseph Smith was in hiding. Knowing the Lord's concern that the work not be stopped for any reason, Joseph gave instructions to the Saints through letters.

In a letter written September 1, 1842, Joseph gave the Saints the Lord's encouragement: "Thus saith the Lord: Let the work of my temple and all the works which I have appointed unto you, be continued on and not cease; and let your diligence, and your perseverance, and patience, and your works be redoubled." (D&C 127:4.)

Five days later, on September 6, 1842, in a letter to the Church, Joseph Smith described the "acceptable offering." Quoting Malachi's prophecy once again concerning the "sons of Levi," Joseph then added this instruction: "Let us, therefore, as a church and a people and as Latter-day Saints, offer unto the Lord an offering in righteousness; and let us present in his holy temple, when it is finished, *a book containing the records of our dead,* which shall be worthy of all *acceptation."* (D&C 128:24; emphasis added.)

At least part of the offering Malachi, John the Baptist, and other prophets had in view was a *book* containing the completed ordinance work for all the dead. It will take the Millennium to achieve that culmination and make it "worthy of all acceptation," for how can the Lord accept it until all of his children who will receive salvation and eternal life have been provided with the opportunity?

As with many prophecies, the offering spoken of has other fulfillments, but it is significant that the one that Lord chose to emphasize in the revelations of the Doctrine and Covenants is that of the work for the dead. Without that offering, the whole earth would be wasted at the Lord's coming.

How appropriate that the offering we are to place on the altars of the temple is a book. It is a fair exchange for the wonderful book our Father in Heaven has placed on those same altars as his offering and gift to us.

In summary, Moroni first quoted the Malachi prophecy and promised that the priesthood would be revealed. John the Baptist next came to begin its revelation and added that the priesthood would remain on the earth until the sons of Levi made an offering in righteousness to the Lord. In section 84, the sons of Levi were identified as all priesthood holders, and it was revealed that the offering would be made in the temple. Finally in Nauvoo, Joseph Smith's letter now recorded as Doctrine and Covenants 128 invited all the Saints to participate in the offering, and the offering was identified. It would be a book containing all the records of ordinance work for the dead. Since that time, tremendous effort and resources have been expended to make the offering "acceptable" to the Lord by completing it.

MANY MODERN INVENTIONS

The Lord is as anxious as our ancestors to help us make our offering and to fulfill the promises. He will help us in many ways. Some we have already discussed, but one of them is unique, enjoyed by all of us and yet comprehended by few—that of modern inventions. What would our lives be like without cars, microwaves, photography, dishwashers, clothes dryers, or computers? Virtually every one of us is grateful for these wonderful conveniences and labor-saving inventions. Their coming forth in such rapid succession in the latter days was not an accident and was not accomplished without the inspiration and direction of the Lord.

Archibald F. Bennett, a prominent genealogist, said, "Sister Susa Young Gates . . . once asked her father [Brigham Young] how it would ever be possible to accomplish the great amount of temple work that must be done, if all are given a full opportunity for exaltation. He told her there would be many inventors of labor-saving devices, so that our daily duties could be performed in a short time, leaving us more and more time for temple work. The inventions have come, and are still coming, but many simply divert the time gained to other channels, and not for the purpose intended by the Lord." (*Improvement Era*, October 1952, p. 720.)

If "the veil were lifted off the face of the Latter-day Saints," Wilford Woodruff taught, and they "could see and know the things of God as they do who are laboring for the salvation of the human family who are in the spirit world . . . , this whole people, with very few, if any, exceptions, would lose all interest in the riches of the world, and instead thereof their whole desires and labors would be directed to redeem their dead." (*Discourses of Wilford Woodruff*, p. 152.) We need to learn to use all the wonderful advances the Lord has inspired in these last days for their truer purposes, not just in our occupations or the earning of a living. Then will we make an acceptable offering in the temples of the Lord.

CHAPTER 18

Promises for the Children

Usually when we read Malachi's prophecy of the return of Elijah, we think of ourselves as the children whose hearts will be turned to our ancestors. But we are also fathers and mothers with children and grandchildren. Does not the temple also turn our hearts to them? Our commitment to the temple and our temple sealings bring blessings upon our posterity. We want the wonderful promises and blessings of the temple to be planted in the hearts of our children. These promises have to do with Godhood and eternal increase. Or, as it was explained to Abraham: "If thou canst count the number of sands, so shall be the number of thy seeds." (Abraham 3:14.)

Joseph F. Smith referred to blessings for the children in his great vision on the redemption of the dead: "The Prophet Elijah was to plant in the hearts of the children the promises made to their fathers, foreshadowing the great work to be done in the temples of the Lord in the dispensation of the fulness of times, for the redemption of the dead, *and the sealing of the children to their parents.*" (D&C 138:47–48; emphasis added.) Notice that both our ancestors and our children are included in Elijah's mission.

Elias's words to Joseph Smith and Oliver Cowdery in the Kirtland Temple also emphasized the blessings upon our children as well as our ancestors. He said "that in us and our seed all generations after us should be blessed." (D&C 110:12.) These blessings have much to do with our marriages in the temple and with the powers and promises that flow to our children because they are "born in the covenant" or are sealed to us.

THE PROMISES OF ETERNAL MARRIAGE

It is appropriate that the pinnacle ordinance of the Restoration, that of temple marriage, was recorded in section 132, one of the last recorded revelations of the Prophet Joseph Smith. Elder Widtsoe's statement quoted earlier indicated that "almost the last words spoken by God to the prophet dealt with the same subject [Elijah's promised return]." In that revelation the final and fullest meaning of "the promises made unto the fathers" is comprehended.

In this revelation, the Lord calls eternal marriage "the law of my Holy Priesthood" and then explains its relationship to Abraham's promises: "Abraham received promises concerning his seed, and of the fruit of his loins—from whose loins ye are, . . . which were to continue so long as they were in the world; and as touching Abraham and his seed, out of the world they should continue; both in the world and out of the world should they continue as innumerable as the stars; or, if ye were to count the sand upon the seashore ye could not number them.

"*This promise is yours also,* because ye are of Abraham, and the promise was made unto Abraham; and *by this law* [eternal marriage or the "law of my Holy Priesthood"] *is the continuation of the works of my Father, wherein he glorifieth himself.*

"Go ye, therefore, and do the works of Abraham; enter ye into my law and ye shall be saved. But if ye enter not into my law ye cannot receive the promise of my Father, which he made unto Abraham." (D&C 132:28–33; emphasis added.)

The promise we can plant in the hearts of our children is the promise of Godhood through the sanctifying ordinances of the temple, particularly that of eternal marriage. Our children's hearts can "turn" to those promises and have faith in their reality. We can teach them to "do the works of Abraham" that they might receive the promise of eternal increase or Godhood that was made to Abraham. Their "seed" will also be as numberless as the stars of heaven or the sands of the seashore.

In our chapels we ordain and set apart people to positions of authority and leadership. We can make a man a stake president or a bishop, but only in the temple can we make eternal families, which leads to Godhood. Our children will not all be bishops, presidents of stakes, or leaders in the auxiliaries, but they can all be Gods, continuing the works of the Father, glorifying themselves as they glorify him. Brigham Young tried to help us catch the power and wonder of this doctrine when he said: "Mankind are organized of element designed to endure to all eternity; it never had a beginning and never can have an end. . . . It is brought together, organized, and capacitated to receive knowledge and intelligence, to be enthroned in glory, to be made angels, Gods—beings who will hold control over the elements, and have power by their word to command the creation and redemption of worlds, or to extinguish suns by their breath, and disorganize worlds, hurling them back into their chaotic state. This is what you and I are created for." (*Journal of Discourses* 3:356.)

What greater or more ennobling promise could be planted in the heart of a child? What greater aspiration, goal, or dignity could you teach a child as a guide to life than the promise that he or she could become like our Father in Heaven? If this promise is planted in our children's hearts, we have given them a powerful source of strength to resist the temptations of Satan and the vain things of the world. They will want to be prepared to enter the temple and secure these blessings for themselves and then secure them for their ancestors.

John the Beloved knew the power of these ideas and used them to encourage the ancient Saints: "Behold, what manner of love the Father hath bestowed upon us, that we should be called the sons of God: therefore the world knoweth us not, because it knew him not. Beloved, now are we the sons of God, and it doth not yet appear what we shall be: but we know that, when he shall appear, *we shall be like him;* for we shall see him as he is. *And every man that hath this hope in him purifieth himself, even as he is pure.*" (1 John 3:1–3; emphasis added.)

THE BURDEN OF THE SCRIPTURES

Now we can understand why Joseph Smith would say: "This doctrine presents in a clear light the wisdom and mercy of God in preparing an ordinance for the salvation of the dead. . . . This doctrine was *the burden of the scriptures.* Those Saints who neglect it in behalf of their deceased relatives, do it at the peril of their own salvation." (*History of the Church* 4:426; emphasis added.) A careful study of the revelations and the history of the Church will show that "the *main concern* of the Prophet Joseph Smith in *the restoration* of the gospel in these latter days was the founding, building, and completion of temples." ("Temple Worship," p. 53.)

We can also comprehend why Brigham Young would say: "We are called, as it has been told you, to redeem the nations of the earth. The fathers cannot be made perfect without us; we cannot be made perfect without the fathers. There must be this chain in the holy Priesthood; it must be welded together from the latest generation that lives on the earth back to Father Adam, to bring back all that can be saved and placed where they can receive salvation and a glory in some kingdom. This Priesthood has to do it; *this Priesthood is for this purpose.*" (*Discourses of Brigham Young,* p. 623; emphasis added.) *Scriptures. Revelation. Restoration. Priesthood. Covenant.* These great key words of the latter days are more closely interwoven with temples than any other gospel subject. Is it not equally important and critical for our own salvation that we plant these sacred temple promises in the hearts of our children?

CHAPTER 19

The Worth of Souls

Early in the Restoration, the Lord told us to "remember the worth of souls is great in the sight of God." (D&C 18:10.) Nothing testifies more to the truth of that pronouncement than our work in the temples for both the living and the dead. When Brigham Young thought of the worth of souls as shown by the Lord's plan for the redemption of the dead, he wished for "a voice like ten thousand earthquakes, that all the world might hear and know the loving kindness of the Lord." (*Discourses of Brigham Young,* p. 626.) As we participate in this work, we too come to understand the depth of the Lord's concern and share his compassion for each individual soul.

GOD HAS NOT FORGOTTEN THEM

While preparing for a tour of Church history and American history sites in the East, our family learned all we could about our American ancestors. We would be visiting areas they came from and wanted the experience to be as positive as it could be. We were going to visit Virginia, and since both my wife and I have family roots there, we spent considerable time trying to learn all the details of these ancestors' lives.

When we found their wills, we discovered that many of them had owned slaves. Most of their wills contained sentences like this: "I give my Negro boy Pompey to my son John and *his heirs forever.*" That phrase struck us deeply, and we felt a yearning through the Spirit to do something for these former slaves. We could not free them from a past earthly bondage, but we felt a compelling desire to free them from a spiritual one.

We allowed our children to help us prepare their names for temple submission, promising that they could be baptized and confirmed for these people when the names were cleared. When we went to the temple to be baptized for them, a wonderful temple worker taught my children something I shall never forget. I believe his words were inspired, for they contained a wisdom and beauty that could come only from a higher source. The experience was especially enlightening because he did not know for whom we were being baptized.

"Many of these people for whom you will be baptized," he said, "lived hard and bitter lives. I am sure that many died thinking God had forgotten them. But you will show them today that he has not forgotten them, that he never forgets a single child. For the first time in many, many years, their names will be spoken again, here in the Lord's house, and they will know of his eternal love for them. And you will show them, also, your own love for them." I have often reflected on his words and thought of all the ordinances that would be completed for Pompey, Lucy, Sal, Mingo, Sookey, Old Tom, and all the other slaves before the work was "acceptable" to the Lord. Their names would be spoken many, many times in their Father's house as each critical ordinance was performed. Hours of ordinance work would be accomplished for each one. They would know of their worth in God's eyes and in their brothers' and sisters' sight.

"I AM WITH MY PEOPLE"

My wife and I were able to perform the endowment for many of these dear black people. With one I felt particularly close. I sensed his eagerness and gratitude through each stage of the endowment. When we entered the celestial room, I felt him whisper in my soul, "Now, finally, I am with my people!"

I knew what he meant. There are no races or nationalities in the temple. There are only the Lord's people, all children of the same Father, all brothers and sisters of the same Christ and of each other, all of tremendous worth to their Father in Heaven. This understanding makes our offering so much more "acceptable." How wonderful it is to hear Samoan brothers speak the names of German immigrants, or Cambodian sisters trying to pronounce Finnish names. "If there is any work in all the world that demonstrates the universality of God's love," taught President Gordon B. Hinckley, "it is the selfless work that goes on in these sacred houses." (*Conference Report,* October 1985, pp. 72–73.)

SAVIORS ON MOUNT ZION

The baptismal font rests securely on the strong backs of twelve oxen. They represent the tribes of Israel, and we belong to those tribes. It is totally appropriate that the font should be so situated. The saving ordinances for the world rest on backs made strong by the blessings of the Restoration. That weight will not be removed until *every child* of God is found. With our heads directed to the four points of the compass, we desire and invite all to receive the ordinances that open the sanctifying power of the Atonement.

My friend's five-year-old son stopped him and his wife as they were going out the door to attend the temple one evening. "Where are you going?" he asked them. "To the temple," they replied. "Well, when you get there, you tell my good friend Jesus hi!" he said. "I don't think we'll see him there, son," his mother replied. "Oh, I think you will see him," he answered, "if you look hard for him."

We have been promised that in the temple, if we are "pure in heart," we "shall see God." (D&C 97:16.) There are many ways of seeing, and some of the most profound do not require our natural eyes. Can we see or understand Jesus any more clearly than when we feel the weight of our brothers' and sisters' salvation, their eternal worth, and share in Jesus' great vicarious work, thus becoming "saviours . . . on mount Zion?" (Obadiah 1:21.) "We have a work to do," Brigham Young said, "just as important in its sphere as the Savior's work was in its sphere. Our fathers cannot be made perfect without us. . . . They have done their work and now sleep. We are now called upon to do ours." (*Discourses of Brigham Young,* p. 623.) In one sense, when we are acting as "saviours on mount Zion," we see with the eyes of the Savior. We see so much more clearly how he viewed all his Father's children, and in that vision we see Jesus more completely.

THE WEIGHT OF GLORY

One of the greatest insights C. S. Lewis received from his study of the scriptures was the conviction that our destiny is to become like God, thus testifying of our tremendous value. When we take a name through the various ordinances, it would be wonderful if we could always be aware of the worth of that name from the eternal point of view.

Lewis described the worth of souls with these words: "The load, or weight, or burden of my neighbor's glory should be laid daily on my back, a load so heavy that only humility can carry it, and the backs of the proud will be broken. It is a serious thing to live in a society of possible gods and goddesses, to remember that the dullest and most uninteresting person you can talk to may one day be a creature which, if you saw it now, you would be strongly tempted to worship. . . . It is in light of these overwhelming possibilities, it is with the awe and circumspection proper to them, that we should conduct all our dealings with one another, all friendships, all loves, all play, all politics. There are no ordinary people. You have never talked to a mere mortal. Nations, cultures, arts, civilizations—these are mortal, and their life is to ours as the life of a gnat. But it is immortals whom we joke with, work with, marry, snub, and exploit. . . . Next to the Blessed Sacrament itself, your neighbor is the holiest object presented to your senses." (From "The Weight of Glory," a sermon given at the Church of St. Mary the Virgin, Oxford.)

If a soul was worth the atoning sacrifice of the Savior, as section 18 teaches us, if it is worth the "whole world" as Jesus taught (Matthew 16:26–29), then surely it is worth hours of our time searching the records for the information necessary to submit the individual names for saving temple ordinances. And if we "labor all [our] days . . . and bring save it be one soul unto [Jesus] how great shall be [our] joy with him in the Kingdom of [our] Father! And now if [our] joy will be great with one soul, . . . how great will be [our] joy if [we] bring many souls." (D&C 18:15–16.)

CHAPTER 20

"A Great and Marvelous Work"

Many times in the early revelations of this dispensation, the Lord introduced his instructions with his own description of the coming work. "A *great* and *marvelous* work is about to come forth among the children of men," he said. (D&C 6:1.) He then invited us to thrust in our sickles and reap the whitened fields. Although his words are true of all the works of the kingdom and are usually applied to missionary work, they are especially true of our labors in the temple.

Surely the work is *great*, especially considering the billions of our Father's children who still await the saving ordinances. But the work is also marvelous. Could there possibly be more whitened fields ready to be harvested than among those who live beyond the veil? We know through the teachings of modern prophets that the work there is different than it is here. Lorenzo Snow assures us, "When the gospel is preached to the spirits in prison, the success attending that preaching will be far greater than that attending the preaching of our elders in this life. I believe there will be very few indeed of those spirits who will not gladly receive the gospel when it is carried to them. The circumstances there will be a thousand times more favorable." (*Millennial Star,* October 6, 1893, p. 718.) I love the Lord's attitude toward this harvest. We need to partake of this spirit as we help our Savior in the work. "If ye have *desires* to serve God," he states, "ye are called to the work." (D&C 4:3; emphasis added.) In other words, the work is so marvelous that the Lord is going to give us the privilege of participating in it with him, but only if we desire to. He does not twist

126

arms or preach duty or try to instill obedience through guilt. He simply tells us that the work itself will be its own reward. In fact, it will be marvelous.

The work is so marvelous that anyone who "thrusteth in his sickle with his might" will reap an eternal and joyful blessing. (D&C 4:4.) Far too often we stress the "greatness" of the work, forgetting its "marvelous" nature. But the Lord himself noted the "marvelous" aspect of the coming work. (See D&C 4:1.) It would be difficult to find anyone who has spent much time in temple work who did not think it was marvelous. May I illustrate with a personal example how I came to understand in a small way how marvelous the work really is?

NAMES WRITTEN IN A BOOK

A few years ago while searching for my Danish ancestors, I was deeply touched as I read the following entries in the Torup parish register. They told the story of Jorgen Larsen and Magrethe Hansdatter, Danish peasants, a story of sorrow and struggle. However, their trials provided me with one of the greatest lessons of my life. Here are the parish church book entries that unfold their lives.

Jorgen Larsen and Magrethe Hansdatter gave birth to a son named Lars, after his paternal grandfather, on November 17, 1776. The child died two weeks later on December 2, 1776. Jorgen and Magrethe gave birth to another son named Lars on May 1, 1778. He died within three weeks, on May 21, 1778. They gave birth to a third son, Hans, named after his maternal grandfather, on August 15, 1779. He died two weeks later, August 29, 1779. On August 20, 1780, Magrethe gave birth to a daughter named Magrethe. This daughter lived seven days and then died on August 27, 1780. A fourth son, Lars, was born October 14, 1781. He died also, on November 18, 1781, after living only a month. A daughter named Karen was born September 7, 1783. She died one week later, on September 14, 1783.

I cannot express the emotions that went through my heart as I followed this account through the pages of the old church book. Finally, on September 5, 1784, Jorgen and Magrethe gave birth to a daughter named Maren, who lived to maturity, and then a son named, appropriately enough, Lars, after his paternal grandfather, on May 26, 1787. This last son was my fourth great-grandfather.

My wife and I went to the Jordan River Temple to seal this family and others as eternal units. The Lord promises us that on occasion we "shall mount up in the imagination of [our] thoughts as upon eagles' wings." (D&C 124:99.) In other words, occasionally he will show us sacred and beautiful truths in the chambers of our minds by touching our imagination. This was one of those occasions. I seemed to see my dear Danish people, all the children gathered around their parents. They were all dressed in white and were rejoicing and embracing each other as the sealings took place. Suddenly, they turned in unison, looking above them at a being I could not see, but I knew who it was by their expressions of gratitude.

"We thank thee, Father," they said, "for allowing us to be born at a time and in a place where our names could be written in a church book, so that our descendant could find our names and bring us here, to thy house, to be cleansed and eternally bound as families. We need wait no longer. *Life is fulfilled.* And we thank thee that our names were written in a book." For temple blessings alone, they dismissed all the pain and struggle of their lives. In spite of their hardships, life was fulfilled by the simple recording of names in a Lutheran church book. Perhaps Paul had these blessings in mind when he told the Roman Saints: "I reckon that the sufferings of this present time are not worthy to be compared with the glory which shall be revealed in us." (Romans 8:18.)

Turning to me with eyes of wonder, my ancestors seemed to say: "And you, our descendant, you are allowed to kneel at an altar in the Lord's house. You have lived your whole life with the assurance of eternal family. You may sit at the feet of living prophets and read words of scripture we never dreamed existed. How full of gratitude your heart must be to our Father in Heaven for all his goodness toward you. For us, it was enough just to have our names written in a church book."

Truly angels descend the Lord's stairway, edifying, instructing, and humbling us as we ascend that same stairway to our eternal home and reunion with them. I can think of no people who have ever lived or who now live that have more reason to rejoice than the Latter-day Saints, for they have had committed to their trust a work that is marvelous in its nature and sanctifying in its performance.

PART 6

HOUSE OF THANKSGIVING

*We pray Thee for the members of Thy Holy Church throughout all the
world, that Thy people may be so guided and governed of Thee, that all who
profess to be and call themselves Saints may be preserved in the unity of the
faith, in the way of truth, in the bonds of peace, and in holiness of life.*

(SALT LAKE TEMPLE DEDICATORY PRAYER.)

CHAPTER 21

The River Rises

I would like to conclude the thoughts I have tried to share on the temple with a testimony. No matter what we read about the temple, our experience there will always be personal. Into each of our lives it will bring unique and beautiful blessings. That is part of its power—it meets our individual needs so perfectly. As its fruits become sweeter in our lives, we feel deep gratitude and realize more fully why the Lord would call the temple "a place of thanksgiving for all saints." (D&C 97:13.) Significantly, the first word of the dedicatory prayer of the Kirtland Temple (the first temple of this dispensation) is the word *thanks*. What more appropriate word could we commence with as a temple is given to the Lord? What wonderful scriptural irony it is that we say "thank you" as we give to God something that will bless us infinitely more than it will bless him.

In quiet moments of reflection, we return often to the temple to express our gratitude. More and more we come to the temple not only for our needs, seeking guidance or comfort, but just to be near the Lord's Spirit and to say, "Thank you." The more we see the temple as a house of learning, a house of refuge, a house of order, and a house of glory, the more we understand why it is also a house of thanksgiving.

In one of the loveliest of psalms, David expressed his love for the Lord because He had "dealt bountifully with" him. Then he asked, "What shall I render unto the Lord for all his benefits toward me?" He then answered his own question: "I will offer to thee *the sacrifice of thanksgiving,* and will call upon the name of the Lord. I will pay my vows unto the Lord now in the presence of all his people, *in the courts of the Lord's house. . . .* Praise ye the Lord." (Psalm 116:7, 12, 17–19; emphasis added.) Temple worship is a beautiful way to thank the Lord for having "dealt bountifully with" us.

I have come to love the temple very much. If someone had told me years ago, when I left the temple after my own endowments, that temple worship would become a central love of my life, I simply would not have believed it was possible. Yet, through the years, I have felt the waters of Ezekiel's river rise continually in my life. I do not know how deeply I have waded into the river. Perhaps I am not even to the knees. But I have felt its refreshing sweetness enough to know that I never want to leave it. The more the river rises, the more grateful I feel to be near enough to wade in it frequently.

I am always thrilled to hear the announcement that another temple will be constructed somewhere in the world. How wonderful that other members will now have easier access to the Lord's house, feel the waters rise in their own lives, and receive their own unique blessings! I believe that the continual building of temples will become more and more critical as the gathering forces of evil begin to prevail in the world. The temples will become a necessity in our lives, and we will feel more and more grateful to enter them frequently.

I would like, by way of testimony, to conclude with three great rewards the temple has brought to my family. I share them as an expression of thanksgiving to the Lord for the goodness that has flowed into my life because of his house. They involve both the temple's healing and its life-giving powers. I hope they will say in the best way possible why I love the Lord's house so deeply.

TURNING THE HEARTS OF THE CHILDREN

When I was just a baby, my parents separated. Not too long after, they divorced. I was raised by my mother, who taught me to love the gospel of Jesus Christ, to search the scriptures, and to trust my Father in Heaven. I rarely saw my father while I grew up. Once a year, while visiting my grandparents, my father would take my sisters and me to Lagoon. That was my only contact with him for the first eighteen years of my life. There was nothing in it upon which one could build a relationship. My father was simply a person who took me to an amusement park once a year. I had no feelings for him, either negative or positive.

When I was eighteen I left California and went to Brigham Young University to attend school. I was deeply interested in genealogy. I enjoyed school, but what I really wanted to do was go to Salt Lake City and spend all day in the Genealogy Library. On the weekends I would hitchhike to Salt Lake City so I could look for my ancestors, but I had to return each night to Provo.

My father lived in Salt Lake City and had a pull-out bed in the couch in his den. I finally called him and asked if I could sleep at his house on Friday and Saturday nights so I could spend more time in the library. Not only did he consent, but he also offered to pick me up in Provo, take me back and forth from the library to his house, and return me to BYU when I was finished.

I loved the weekends and looked forward to them all week long. I tried to get all my homework done so I would have the full weekend to spend in Salt Lake City. I never could have foreseen what those weekend trips would eventually lead to. At night I would talk with my father and show him what I had found. I learned to like him, and then I learned to love him. My heart was turning. The first father that Elijah's spirit caused me to turn to was not some distant ancestor I would meet someday in the resurrection. It was my own father.

Time passed, and I shared many more memories with my father. A desire was born in my heart to help him return to full activity in the Church. Years passed, and progress was sometimes slow and discouraging, but the day finally came when I received a call from my father and heard him say: "Do you know what I am holding in my hand? It is a temple recommend. I am worthy to return to the Lord's house. It's been over thirty years. Would you come to Salt Lake City and go with me?" What a sweet experience awaited my sister and me as we entered the Jordan River Temple with our father.

Since that day, my father has been to the temple many times. I have continued to do research on our ancestors. I submit their names for temple ordinances, and my father is in the temple every week performing the work for them. I do not doubt the power of Malachi's promise. The spirit of Elijah can reach through centuries of time and bind our hearts to fathers whose names we read on old gothic manuscripts, but it can also reach through the pain of divorce and bind the heart of a son to his father and a father to his son. That is one of the great rewards I have received because Elijah came to fulfill Malachi's promise.

What Shall Thy Wages Be?

When I was a boy, I fell onto the cement and cracked the upper ridge of my mouth. We were unaware of this until many years later when an X-ray revealed the damage. By then it was too late to save the front teeth. While a teenager, I had several operations. My front teeth were removed, and braces were attached to correct the damage. During years of corrective brace work, I lived with a toothless smile. These were my high school years.

I learned to talk without ever showing my teeth. I don't recall this as a great hardship, but it did result in a complete lack of confidence socially. I never dated, and I had very little to do with girls. I recall entering the mission field with a great sense of relief that I would have two whole years without needing to worry about social contacts or dating.

I reached maturity believing I could not and would not marry a wonderful woman. I accepted this knowledge as a part of life and was resigned to settle down with a wife who was less than what I wanted. Yet I had dreams. I had formed a portrait of a perfect wife down to the tiniest details—her talents, her personality, her life's commitments, what she would look like, even to the color of her hair and eyes. It was a dream I did not believe could ever come true.

The scriptures teach that the Lord honors his sons by giving them wonderful wives. (Proverbs 19:14.) If that is true, then surely no man was ever honored more than I. Laura Chipman came into my life possessing every detail of my portrait, even to the color of her hair and eyes.

Perhaps you can understand, then, how I felt as I knelt in the Alberta Temple, heard the wonderful words of promise and fulfillment that were spoken there, and knew that this unity and love, which I had never believed would come into my life, would now never leave it if I would remain true to my covenants.

As she placed her hand in mine while we knelt at the altar, such a warmth of spirit and light and beauty rolled over and around and through me that ever since that time, whenever I hear the word *glory*, I think of that moment. At the altars of the temple, the Lord opens a window of heaven just a crack to let celestial light strike our souls as a taste of what can be ours forever if we are true to our covenants. I had never before nor have I ever since felt such an elation of pure joy.

A thought by Arthur Henry King has meant much to me since I read it years ago. He said: "I was born extremely poor, but I had no ambitions; and I was surprised every time something good happened to me. And I continue to be so. What one doesn't expect may prove to be a source of gratitude, and gratitude is a fundamental gospel attitude. It is what we have to feel; we have to give it back to the Lord in all things." (*The Abundance of the Heart,* p. 78.)

I never expected to have a strong relationship with my father, nor did I expect the sweetness of a wonderful companion, but the Lord's house not only brought these things into my life but also assures me that they can be eternal. What other feeling could be more appropriate than gratitude? When I first went to the temple, I did not expect it to provide such fulfillment and joy. I doubt that many of us can comprehend at first what the temple really can do for us. Perhaps that is why our hearts swell wider and wider with gratitude as the blessings flow and our lives become richer and richer.

I love the story of Jacob and Rachel in the Old Testament. I think it is the most profoundly beautiful love story in literature, yet it covers only a few verses. "Because thou art my brother," Laban asked Jacob, "shouldest thou therefore serve me for nought? Tell me, what shall thy wages be?"

And Jacob answered, "I will serve thee seven years for Rachel thy younger daughter." The seven years turned into fourteen, but we are told the years "seemed unto him but a few days, for the love he had to her." (Genesis 29:15–20.)

I can picture a similar scene in my own life sometime in the future. My Father in Heaven will ask me a question much like the one Laban asked Jacob: "Because thou art my son, shouldest thou, therefore, serve me for nought? Tell me, What shall thy wages be?"

I know what answer I will give him. I will not ask for a mansion in heaven, but I will ask for an even greater reward. Yet I know it is one he desires to grant me. "I will serve thee all my life," I will answer, "for the eternal companionship of thy daughter Laura. Please seal my marriage with thy Holy Spirit of Promise. Preserve the fruit, Father, we have gathered in our lives together." What greater reward could one ask than that?

Wilford Woodruff understood this truth, for he loved his wife dearly. "Bless your souls," he said, "if you lived here in the flesh a thousand years, as long as Father Adam, and lived and labored all your life in poverty, and when you got through, if, by your acts, you could secure your wives and children in the morning of the first resurrection, to dwell with you in the presence of God, that one thing would amply pay you for the labors of a thousand years." (*Journal of Discourses* 21:284.)

THEY KEPT COMING AND COMING

I took my twelve-year-old son to the temple one afternoon to perform baptisms for a number of his ancestors. He had gone with me a number of times to the Family History Library and had, on his own, found some of his ancestors. This was not the first time we had gone together to the temple to be baptized for the dead, but it turned out to be one of the most special. There was a beautiful, calm spirit in the temple that afternoon. We performed the baptisms and then the confirmations. After he was confirmed for his ancestors, he told me of a special experience he had received during the confirmations. It said so much about the wonder of the temple and the gratitude it engenders.

He said: "When the workers laid their hands on my head, I saw a picture in my mind. I saw you, Dad, standing alone. Then Mother came and stood by you and took your hand. Then Kirsten, Megan, Ben, Mckay, and I came, and we stood with you. I saw Grandma and Grandpa come next and join us. Then people began to come from many different directions. I did not know who they were, but they came and stood with us and took our hands. They kept coming and coming until I could not see the end of them."

What sweeter moment could a father share with his son than I shared with mine that afternoon in the temple of our God? What gratitude it continues to create in my heart as I reflect on it. One day my son will know who all the people were, and the experience described by Enoch will be his also: "Then shalt thou and all thy city meet them there, and we will receive them into our bosom, and they shall see us; and we will fall upon their necks, and they shall fall upon our necks, and we will kiss each other." (Moses 7:63.) The essence of the temple is contained in that verse. May the experience it describes be the reward of all who truly love the Lord's house.

SHOUT FOR JOY

As I reflect on all the joy the temple has brought into my life and the strength it gives every member of the Church, it is not difficult to understand why we shout for joy when a temple is dedicated. That holy, solemn occasion is such a fitting celebration of the happiness that the newly dedicated temple will bring to all who pass through its door.

I have been privileged to participate in the dedication of three temples. Each one was a sacred occasion I shall always remember and treasure. Only on the most holy occasions of real joy do we shout because our happiness is so full we must let it out in praise to our Father and his Son. The scriptures speak of only a few such occasions. Job taught that "the morning stars sang together, and all the sons of God *shouted* for joy" when the earth was created. (Job 38:7; emphasis added.) Joseph Smith quoted Job's shout of joy in his great hymn of the Restoration spoken of in an earlier chapter. (See D&C 128:23.)

When Jesus triumphantly entered Jerusalem to accomplish his great redeeming sacrifice for the salvation of the world, the streets were lined with people who "began to rejoice and praise God with a loud voice." (Luke 19:37.) "Hosanna!" they cried. "Blessed is the King of Israel that cometh in the name of the Lord." (John 12:13.) Zechariah described this triumphant promise of the coming Atonement with these words: "Rejoice greatly, O daughter of Zion; *shout* O daughter of

Jerusalem: behold thy King cometh unto thee." (Zechariah 9:9; emphasis added.)

Paul informed the Thessalonians that when the Savior returned to the earth, he would "descend from heaven with a *shout* . . . and the dead in Christ shall rise." (1 Thessalonians 4:16; emphasis added.) All of these moments are deeply significant in the salvation of humanity. The Creation, the coming Atonement, and the Resurrection are all occasions for shouting "hosanna to God and the Lamb!" It is not coincidental that the dedication of the Lord's house is also accompanied by a shout of rejoicing, for it too is essential in the salvation of our Father's children. May that shout echo again and again in every land, among every people, and sound in every ear.

Bibliography

American Heritage Dictionary. Boston: Houghton Mifflin Co., 1982.

Benson, Ezra Taft. *The Teachings of Ezra Taft Benson.* Salt Lake City: Bookcraft, 1988.

Bolt, Robert. *A Man for All Seasons.* New York: Scholastic Book Services, 1960.

Cannon, George Q. *Gospel Truth.* Selected by Jerreld L. Newquist. Salt Lake City: Deseret Book Company, 1987.

Derrick, Royden G. *Temples in the Last Days.* Salt Lake City: Bookcraft, 1987.

Farrar, Frederic. *The Life of Christ.* Salt Lake City: Bookcraft, 1994.

Grant, Heber J. *Gospel Standards.* Compiled by G. Homer Durham. Salt Lake City: Improvement Era, 1941.

Hinckley, Bryant S. *Sermons and Missionary Services of Melvin Joseph Ballard.* Salt Lake City: Deseret Book Company, 1949.

Journal of Discourses. 26 vols. London: Latter-day Saints' Book Depot, 1854–86.

Kimball, Spencer W. *The Teachings of Spencer W. Kimball.* Salt Lake City: Bookcraft, 1982.

King, Arthur Henry. *The Abundance of the Heart.* Salt Lake City: Bookcraft, 1986.

MacDonald, George. *An Anthology.* Edited by C. S. Lewis. New York: Macmillan Publishing Company, 1978.

———. *The Gifts of the Child Christ.* Grand Rapids, Mich.: William B. Eerdmans Publishing Co., 1973.

Melvin J. Ballard: Crusader for Righteousness. Salt Lake City: Bookcraft, 1966.

Packer, Boyd K. *The Holy Temple.* Salt Lake City: Bookcraft, 1980.

Sandburg, Carl. *Abraham Lincoln: The Prairie Years and the War Years.* New York: Harcourt, Brace & World, 1954.

Seeking After Our Dead (Salt Lake City: Genealogical Society of Utah, 1928).

Smith, Joseph. *Teachings of the Prophet Joseph Smith.* Selected by Joseph Fielding Smith. Salt Lake City: Deseret Book Company, 1938.

———. *History of The Church of Jesus Christ of Latter-day Saints.* 7 vols. 2nd ed. rev.

141

Edited by B. H. Roberts. Salt Lake City: The Church of Jesus Christ of Latter-day Saints, 1932–51.

Smith, Joseph F. *Gospel Doctrine.* 5th ed. Salt Lake City: Deseret Book Company, 1939.

Talmage, James E. *The House of the Lord.* Salt Lake City: Deseret Book Company, 1971.

The New Strong's Exhaustive Concordance of the Bible. Nashville: Thomas Nelson Publishers, 1984.

Widtsoe, John A. "Temple Worship." *Utah Genealogical and Historical Magazine,* 12 (April 1921): 64.

————. *In a Sunlit Land.* Salt Lake City: Deseret News Press, 1952.

Wilson's Old Testament Word Studies. Mclean, Va.: MacDonald Publishing Co., n.d.

Woodruff, Wilford. *Discourses of Wilford Woodruff.* Selected by G. Homer Durham. Salt Lake City: Bookcraft, 1946.

Young, Brigham. *Discourses of Brigham Young.* Selected by John A. Widtsoe. Salt Lake City: Deseret Book Company, 1941.

Index

143